Life-Study of Genesis

Messages 110-120

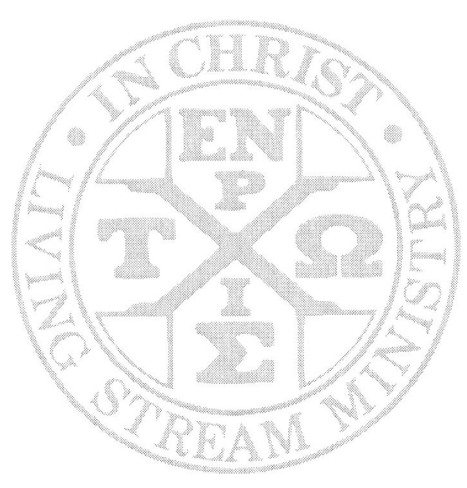

Witness Lee

Living Stream Ministry
Anaheim, CA • www.lsm.org

© 1978 Living Stream Ministry

All rights reserved. No part of this work may be reproduced or transmitted in any form or by any means—graphic, electronic, or mechanical, including photocopying, recording, or information storage and retrieval systems—without written permission from the publisher.

First Edition, August 1997.

ISBN 978-0-7363-0836-6
(Complete set, softcover)
ISBN 978-0-87083-916-0
(Messages 110-120, softcover)

Published by

Living Stream Ministry
2431 W. La Palma Ave., Anaheim, CA 92801 U.S.A.
P. O. Box 2121, Anaheim, CA 92814 U.S.A.

Printed in the United States of America

13 14 15 16 17 18 / 13 12 11 10 9 8 7

CONTENTS

MESSAGE ONE HUNDRED TEN BEING MATURED THE REIGNING ASPECT OF THE MATURED ISRAEL (1) PAGE 1405

3) The Reigning Aspect of the Matured Israel — a) Joseph's Life — Being the Generation of Jacob — b) Joseph Being a Type of Christ — (1) A Shepherd — (2) The Father's Beloved — (3) Ministering to the Brothers according to the Father's Will — (4) Hated and Harassed by the Brothers to Whom He Ministers — (5) Viewing His People as Sheaves of Life and as the Sun, the Moon, and the Stars of Light — (6) His People to Be under His Reign

MESSAGE ONE HUNDRED ELEVEN JOSEPH'S LIVING CORRESPONDING WITH HIS VISION PAGE 1421

    I. LIVING AS A SHEAF OF LIFE   (1423)

        A. His Brothers Giving Vent to Their Anger — B. Joseph Emerging from Anger, Surviving in a Death Situation

    II. LIVING AS A STAR OF LIGHT   (1426)

        A. His Brother Judah Indulging in Lust — B. Joseph Overcoming Lust, Shining in Darkness

    III. LIVING THE KINGDOM LIFE   (1428)

    IV. ENJOYING THE LORD'S PRESENCE   (1429)

        A. Prospered by the Lord — B. The Favor with the Lord's Blessing

| MESSAGE ONE HUNDRED TWELVE | BEING MATURED THE REIGNING ASPECT OF THE MATURED ISRAEL (2) | PAGE 1431 |

(7) Betrayed — (8) Delivered into the Prison of Death

I. JOSEPH TRIED BY HIS DREAMS NOT BEING FULFILLED (1436)

II. JOSEPH HAVING THE FAITH AND THE BOLDNESS TO INTERPRET THE DREAMS OF HIS TWO COMPANIONS IN PRISON (1437)

III. JOSEPH CONFIRMED AND STRENGTHENED BY THE FULFILLMENT OF THE DREAMS OF HIS COMPANIONS IN PRISON (1439)

IV. JOSEPH TRIED FURTHER BY HIS DREAMS NOT BEING FULFILLED FOR ANOTHER PERIOD OF TIME (1440)

| MESSAGE ONE HUNDRED THIRTEEN | BEING MATURED THE REIGNING ASPECT OF THE MATURED ISRAEL (3) | PAGE 1445 |

(9) Resurrected from the Prison of Death — (10) Enthroned with Authority — (11) Receiving Glory — (12) Receiving Gifts — (13) Becoming the Savior of the World, the Sustainer of Life (the Revealer of Secrets) — (14) Taking the Church — (15) Supplying People with Food

| MESSAGE ONE HUNDRED FOURTEEN | THE SECRET OF JOSEPH'S RELEASE AND EXALTATION | PAGE 1457 |

I. JOSEPH BECOMING QUALIFIED IN AGE AFTER THE FURTHER SUFFERING OF TWO YEARS (1457)

II. JOSEPH RELEASED FROM PRISON INDIRECTLY THROUGH HIS INTERPRETATION OF THE CUPBEARER'S DREAM (1459)

III. JOSEPH GIVEN AUTHORITY DIRECTLY THROUGH HIS INTERPRETATION OF PHARAOH'S DREAMS (1461)

IV. JOSEPH MINISTERING FOOD TO PEOPLE THROUGH HIS INTERPRETATION OF DREAMS (1462)

V. JOSEPH'S LIFE BEING A LIFE OF DREAMS (1463)

| MESSAGE ONE HUNDRED FIFTEEN | BEING MATURED THE REIGNING ASPECT OF THE MATURED ISRAEL (4) | PAGE 1469 |

(16) Recognized by the Children of Israel — (a) The Whole Earth Being under Famine — (b) Food Being Only Where Christ Is — (c) The Children of Israel Forced to Turn to Christ — (d) Ignorant concerning Christ — (e) Christ Testing Them — (f) Christ Disciplining Them — (g) Christ Showing Love to Them — (h) Ignorant of Christ's Love

| MESSAGE ONE HUNDRED SIXTEEN | JOSEPH'S DEALING WITH HIS BROTHERS | PAGE 1477 |

I. JOSEPH NOT OUT OF CONTROL IN SEEING HIS DREAMS FULFILLED (1477)

II. JOSEPH NOT HASTY TO SHOW HIS GLORY TO HIS BROTHERS (1478)

III. JOSEPH BEING WISE IN DEALING WITH HIS BROTHERS (1479)

A. Causing Them to Realize Their Guilt in Hating and Selling Him — B. Disciplining Simeon — C. Testing Them with Respect to Benjamin

IV. JOSEPH SHOWING LOVE TO HIS BROTHERS (1482)

| MESSAGE ONE HUNDRED SEVENTEEN | BEING MATURED THE REIGNING ASPECT OF THE MATURED ISRAEL (5) | PAGE 1489 |

(i) The Children of Israel Further Forced to Turn to Christ — (j) Still Being Ignorant of Christ — (k) Christ Showing More Love to Them — (l) Still Being Ignorant of Christ's Love

| MESSAGE ONE HUNDRED EIGHTEEN | BEING MATURED THE REIGNING ASPECT OF THE MATURED ISRAEL (6) | PAGE 1501 |

(m) Christ Giving the Remnant of Israel the Last Test — (n) Still Remaining Ignorant of Him — (o) Christ Acknowledging the Ignorant Israel — (p) Eventually Recognizing Christ

| MESSAGE ONE HUNDRED NINETEEN | BEING MATURED THE REIGNING ASPECT OF THE MATURED ISRAEL (7) | PAGE 1511 |

(q) Christ's Revealing His Exaltation and Glory to Repentant Israel —
(r) Israel Participating in the Enjoyment of Christ's Reign

| MESSAGE ONE HUNDRED TWENTY | BEING MATURED THE REIGNING ASPECT OF THE MATURED ISRAEL (8) | PAGE 1523 |

(17) Reigning — (a) Supplying People with Food — (b) Keeping People Alive — (c) Keeping the Land Producing — (d) Taking Special Care of Israel

LIFE-STUDY OF GENESIS

MESSAGE ONE HUNDRED TEN

BEING MATURED
THE REIGNING ASPECT OF THE MATURED ISRAEL

(1)

Genesis is a wonderful book. The more we study it, the more we realize that no human hand could have written it. Apparently Genesis is simply a book of stories; however, when we probe into the depths of this book through the guidance of the Holy Spirit, we find that it contains something profound related to our experience of life. If we read superficially, we shall not be able to understand why the events of chapter thirty-eight are put after those of chapter thirty-seven. Not until we discover the spiritual significance of these chapters can we appreciate the deep meaning of their sequence.

According to the record of the book of Genesis and according to our spiritual experience, Joseph should not be considered a person separate from Jacob, but rather as an aspect of Jacob's biography. When we first came to Abraham in this life-study, we pointed out that, in spiritual experience, Abraham, Isaac, and Jacob are not three separate individuals. Instead, they represent three aspects of the experience of one saint. Abraham, Isaac, and Jacob represent three aspects of one spiritual man, and their biographies portray different aspects of the complete life of a saint. Abraham, Isaac, and Jacob are three aspects of one person, somewhat like the Father, the Son, and the Spirit are the three of the Godhead. In the record of Genesis, God revealed Himself as the God of Abraham, the God of Isaac, and the God of Jacob. But the God of Abraham, Isaac, and Jacob is not three separate Gods; He is one Triune God. In a similar way, spiritually speaking, Abraham, Isaac, and Jacob are not three separate persons, but three aspects of one complete person. Therefore, we have not only the Triune God, but also a complete man of three aspects.

It is difficult to determine whether Abraham or Jacob comes first. According to the historical record, Abraham was the grandfather, and Jacob was the grandson. According to spiritual experience, however, Jacob must come first. Jacob was chosen before he was born (Rom. 9:11-13). This means that the complete saint was chosen as Jacob before birth. The book of Ephesians reveals that this selection took place before the foundation of the world (Eph. 1:4). Thus, the complete person was chosen as Jacob. He was also fallen as Jacob. Then this chosen and fallen one was called as Abraham. With Abraham, he not only was called, but also was justified and lived a life by faith. Furthermore, he inherited and enjoyed all the riches of Christ as Isaac. After he had been called and justified, and while he was living a life by faith, he inherited all the riches of Christ and enjoyed them. But this is not all. As Jacob, he also struggled and suffered because of his strivings. Moreover, he was dealt with and became matured. All this is the experience of Jacob. For all these experiences—the choosing, the fall, the calling, the justification by faith, the living by faith, the inheritance and enjoyment of the riches in Christ, the self-struggling, the sufferings, the dealings, and the maturity—there is the need of three persons, the need of Abraham, Isaac, and Jacob.

These three represent you and me. We are chosen and fallen as Jacob. We are called, we are justified by faith, and we live by faith as Abraham. We inherit the riches of Christ and enjoy them as Isaac. We struggle, suffer, are dealt with, and mature as Jacob. When Jacob was matured, his name was changed. Not only was his disposition transformed, but his name was changed from Jacob, a supplanter, to Israel, a matured prince of God, one who could reign for God.

3) The Reigning Aspect of the Matured Israel

The matured Israel has a reigning aspect. We have seen the process of Jacob's maturity and the manifestation of his maturity. His maturity was fully manifested in his excellent departure from this life. Now we must see the reigning aspect of this matured life. Therefore, in this message we come to the reigning aspect of the matured Israel, an aspect fully portrayed in the biography of Joseph.

Because Joseph represents an aspect of Jacob, we should not consider Joseph a person separate from Jacob. This is the reason the last fourteen chapters of Genesis combine the record of Joseph's life with the record of Jacob's. Genesis blends the biographies of Joseph and Jacob because they are actually the biography not of two persons, but of one. This blending of the record indicates that Joseph is an aspect of Jacob. If you read the record in Genesis from chapter thirty-seven through chapter fifty, you will see that Joseph is an aspect, a part, of Jacob. He was Jacob's expression. Wherever Joseph was, Jacob was there also. When Joseph was in power, it was actually Jacob who was reigning. Hence, their biographies are blended together as the biography of one person.

For years I tried to divide each of the books of the Bible into sections. But when I came to the last chapters of the book of Genesis, I could not tell whether it was a section pertaining to Jacob or to Joseph. Eventually I gave up trying to divide this part of Genesis into sections. Because at that time I did not see the matter of life, I did not appreciate the excellence of the composition of Genesis. But we need to recognize that these chapters are part of one biography with two aspects. The day I saw this light I was very happy. Spiritually speaking, Joseph is not separate from Jacob. Rather, he represents the reigning aspect of a matured saint.

a) Joseph's Life—Being the Generation of Jacob

Genesis 37:2 says, "These are the generations of Jacob." Then it goes on to tell us of the life of Joseph. This proves that Joseph's life was a part of Jacob's generation. Joseph's biography is an aspect of Jacob's history.

b) Joseph Being a Type of Christ

Joseph's biography indicates that he had no defects. According to the record, he was altogether perfect. In the Bible Joseph is the perfect one in the Old Testament, and Jesus is the perfect One in the New Testament. The four biographies of Jesus in the New Testament reveal that He was perfect, without defect. The record of Joseph in the Old Testament reveals that he also was perfect. Some may say that in order to be a type of Christ, Joseph had to be perfect. But was not David a type of Christ? Certainly he was. But David, a type of Christ, committed gross sin. Solomon also was a type of Christ, but he too was sinful. With the exception of Joseph, all the personal types of Christ in the Old Testament had some shortcomings.

As a type of Christ, Joseph signifies the reigning aspect of a matured saint, the mature Israel. Certainly the reigning aspect of such a person must be perfect. None of us, of course, is perfect. However, in our reigning aspect we are perfect. Whenever we are reigning in the spirit, we are perfect. Nevertheless, you may say, "I am not perfect. Rather, I am like Judah." However, the aspect of you which is like Judah is not your reigning aspect, but your fallen aspect. Yes, according to your fallen aspect you are like Judah in chapter thirty-eight. Both chapters thirty-seven and thirty-nine are chapters of perfection. Chapter thirty-eight, on the contrary, is a chapter of perversion. Thus, the reigning aspect is in chapter thirty-seven and the fallen aspect in chapter thirty-eight. Perhaps yesterday you were reigning for God, but today you may have committed sin, even a gross sin. This reveals the fact that we have various aspects. In this message we shall deal only with the reigning aspect.

I hope that we all shall see that Abraham, Isaac, and Jacob with Joseph are one person. Joseph is not a separate aspect of a complete spiritual person as Abraham, Isaac, and Jacob are. Rather, as we have seen, Joseph is an aspect of Jacob. The Bible does not say that God is the God of Abraham, the God of Isaac, the God of Jacob, and the God of Joseph. This would make God quaternary instead of triune. There are only three. But when we come in Jacob to the stage of maturity, we see that with the mature life there is the reigning aspect. Neither Abraham nor Isaac reigned. But Joseph reigned representatively for Jacob. In other words, Jacob reigned through Joseph.

In 1:26, when God created man, He said, "Let us make man in our image, after our likeness: and let them have dominion...." In the last few chapters of Genesis we see an Israel expressing God's image and exercising His dominion. The exercise of God's dominion over all things is manifested in Joseph's life, whereas God's image is expressed in Israel. Joseph is not separate from Jacob, but is an aspect of the life that expresses God's image. The two aspects of expressing God's image and exercising God's dominion must be found in one person. Therefore, what is found in Joseph's life may be called the reigning aspect of the matured Israel. Without this light, you will not be able to understand this portion of the Word. Sorry to say, most Christians do not have this light.

Our goal must be to express God with His image and to represent Him with His dominion. For this, we are chosen and fallen as Jacob; we are called, we are justified, and we live by faith as Abraham; we inherit the riches of Christ and enjoy them as Isaac; and finally we struggle, we suffer, we are dealt with, and we reach maturity as Jacob. We all have the "Jacobean" struggling nature within us. If we were told not to struggle, we would struggle just the same. Struggling, however, is not necessarily wrong. If one has been a Christian for years but has never struggled, it means that he is not one who is seeking the Lord. It also means that he is not interested in gaining the birthright. But once we realize something about the birthright, we shall struggle to be holy and spiritual, and our "Jacobean" struggling nature will come out. When you struggle, be prepared to suffer. Along with the suffering, you will be under God's dealing hand. You may be smart, but God has a Laban who is smarter than you are. Be prepared to suffer and to be dealt with by the hand of God. Eventually you will reach maturity, and the reigning aspect of the matured Israel will be seen in your life. This is the reigning aspect represented by Joseph.

Again I say, Joseph is not a complete person, but simply an aspect of a matured saint who has passed through the experiences represented by the lives of Abraham, Isaac, and Jacob. After passing through all these experiences, the matured saint has an aspect that is constituted solely of

Christ. Because this aspect of him is the constitution of Christ, it is perfect. Joseph represents this constituted aspect of a matured saint. In each of us there is a part that is constituted of Christ. Even if you have just been regenerated, a part of you, your regenerated spirit, has been constituted of Christ. This is the beginning of Christ's constitution in you. The process of being constituted of Christ will continue until it reaches its climax when the reigning aspect comes forth in you. When you are fully matured, you will have this top portion, this top aspect. This is the constitution of Christ, an aspect of the mature life constituted of Christ.

No doubt, Joseph is the perfect type of Christ because he portrays the constituted aspect of a mature saint. If the aspect of you which is constituted of Christ is not perfect, then surely no part of you could be perfect. In us who are fallen, saved, called, redeemed, and regenerated there is nothing perfect except the constituting Christ. Hallelujah, we have Christ's constitution within us! I repeat, Joseph represents the constitution of Christ in Jacob's mature life. This aspect, Christ constituted in the matured saints, is perfect. Hence, it perfectly typifies Christ.

(1) A Shepherd

This perfect aspect is a shepherd. Joseph, like Abel, was a shepherd (37:2). This typifies the aspect of the constitution of Christ in the mature life that is the shepherding life to take care of others. In chapter thirty-seven Joseph not only fed and shepherded the flock; although he was the second youngest brother, he was sent by his father to shepherd his brothers. Thus, Joseph shepherded not only his father's flock, but also his father's sons. The Lord Jesus also came as a shepherd (John 10:11).

Although you may be new in the church life, you nevertheless have the constitution of Christ within you. Christ has been constituted into you, and this becomes the constitution of Christ in your spiritual life. This is what gives you the burden to take care of others. This is shepherding. The constitution of Christ in our spiritual life has a shepherding aspect. It is vain to encourage people to shepherd others. The more I charge you to shepherd others, the less you will shepherd them. Shepherding is not a matter of our instigating others to do something, but of Christ's constitution within them. The part of our being that has been constituted of Christ is the part that shepherds others. I have full confidence in that part of you. We cannot shepherd anyone, but Christ constituted into us is the Shepherd.

The reigning aspect is firstly the shepherding aspect. If you do not have the burden to shepherd others and to feed them, you will never be able to reign. Reigning authority comes from the shepherding life. Eventually, Joseph reigned over his brothers. But he did not reign over them until he had already shepherded them. He was sent by his father to shepherd his brothers and to feed them. In like manner, Jesus came not as a King to rule others; He came as a Shepherd.

As the Shepherd, Christ was killed by His own people. This is revealed in John 10, where we are told that the good Shepherd gives His life for the sheep. Jesus came as the Shepherd and was killed, giving His life for His flock. In principle, the same thing happened to Joseph in chapter thirty-seven. Although he was sent to shepherd his brothers, they nearly killed him. Joseph gave his life in order to carry out this kind of shepherding. It is good that we have a shepherding life within. But if you are to shepherd others, you must be ready to be killed by those you are caring for. The very ones you desire to shepherd will not appreciate your shepherding. Instead, they will kill you. They may think of you as a strange, peculiar person, and they may call you a "holy" brother. Many have said to me, "Brother Lee, if I stay by myself and do not love the church and care for the saints, I have no problems. But when I begin to love the church and take care of the saints, the saints kill me." They kill you because you shepherd them.

(2) The Father's Beloved

Joseph, the one with the shepherding aspect, was also his father's beloved (37:3-4). Likewise, Christ was the Father's beloved Son (Matt. 3:17; 17:5). Only that aspect of us that is constituted of Christ is beloved in the eyes of God. Praise the Lord that we have Christ's constitution within us! This part of us is beloved of the Father. You can testify that at times you have had the deep sense that the Father was present with you, and you could sense Him saying, "This is My beloved." The words spoken of the Lord Jesus at His baptism and on the Mount of Transfiguration have also been spoken to you. You have had the deep sense that God the Father was present. Whenever you have this sense, it is a proof that you have the constitution of Christ, which is pleasing to the Father. Of that part of your being the Father will always say, "This is My beloved."

Although you may be young in the Lord, I believe that you have experienced the Father God in heaven being very happy with you and pleased with you. However, now you may not be pleased with yourself, considering your shortcomings and faults. The reason for this is that we have two constitutions, the constitution of Christ and the constitution of the old Adam. When you are with the constitution of Christ, you can hear a heavenly voice saying, "This is My beloved," because God the Father is pleased with you. But when you are with the old constitution, the constitution of Adam, not even you are pleased with yourself. Rather, you hate that aspect of your being. Joseph represents the very constitution of Christ in the matured life of Israel, that part which is called by the Father, "My beloved."

(3) Ministering to the Brothers according to the Father's Will

In 37:12-17 we see that Joseph ministered to the brothers according to his father's will. In this matter also Joseph was a type of Christ, for Christ came down from heaven to do the will of the One who had sent Him (John 6:38).

There is not a word in the Bible saying that Joseph was a type of Christ. However, if you read this section of the Word, you will admit not only that Joseph was a type of Christ, but that his biography is virtually the biography of Christ. Joseph's life was a copy of Christ's.

At this point I would like to say a word regarding allegorizing the Bible. Some Bible teachers say that we should consider as types only those things in the Old Testament that the New Testament specifically says are types. I followed this teaching for a number of years, but I was eventually released from it, having realized that it went too far. Although there is not a word in the New Testament saying that Joseph was a type of Christ, no one in the Old Testament was a more exact type of Christ than Joseph was. This indicates the fact that some things in the Old Testament are types which are not referred to as types in the New Testament. Because of this fact, I no longer hold this teaching. Joseph was a shepherd, the father's beloved, and the one sent by the father to minister to his brothers. In all these aspects he was the same as Christ.

(4) Hated and Harassed
by the Brothers to Whom He Ministers

Although Joseph was a shepherd and the father's beloved and although he ministered to his brothers according to his father's will, he was hated and harassed by the brothers to whom he ministered (37:4-5, 8, 11, 18-36). The same was true of Christ (Acts 10:38-39). Christ was sent to minister to the children of God, but they hated Him. According to the Gospels, the Jewish leaders hated Christ, conspired against Him, and plotted to kill Him. This was also Joseph's experience with his brothers. In 37:19 and 20 his brothers said, "Behold, this master of dreams cometh. Come now therefore, and let us slay him..." (Heb.). Thus, they conspired and plotted against their brother Joseph.

Joseph's brothers harassed him through the Ishmaelites, who were Midianites (37:25, 28). Both the Ishmaelites and the Midianites were descendants of Abraham. Abraham had three wives: Sarah, Hagar, and Keturah. Through Sarah, his genuine wife, Abraham brought forth Isaac. Through Hagar, Sarah's handmaid, he brought forth Ishmael, the product of Abraham's flesh. Finally, through Keturah, Abraham brought forth Midian. Only one son—Isaac—was brought forth by grace. Both Ishmael and Midian were brought forth through the flesh. Therefore, in the Old Testament both Ishmael and Midian signify the flesh, the natural strength. Joseph, a descendant of Isaac, was sold to the descendants of Ishmael and Midian, to the Ishmaelites, the Midianites. It seems that the Bible erroneously uses the terms the Ishmaelites and the Midianites interchangeably. In chapter thirty-seven, verse 25 speaks of the Ishmaelites and verse 28, of the Midianites. Were the ones to whom Joseph was sold Ishmaelites or Midianites? According to the Bible, both the Ishmaelites and the Midianites were of the same category. In the eyes of God the Ishmaelites and the Midianites both signify the flesh. Thus, Joseph was sold through the flesh. The same thing happened to the Lord Jesus. If the Jewish leaders had been in the spirit, they would never have delivered Jesus Christ to Pilate. Christ was delivered to Pilate by the Jewish leaders through the flesh. When the Jewish leaders delivered Jesus to Pilate, they were no longer Israelites; they were Ishmaelites and Midianites. Their delivering up of the Lord Jesus was done in the flesh.

Joseph was sold through the flesh to Egypt (37:28, 36), which signifies the world. The fact that Joseph was sold through the flesh to the world indicates that the flesh is linked to the world. It was the same in the case of the Lord Jesus. Through the flesh, the Jewish leaders delivered Christ to Pilate, the Roman authority, who certainly was in Egypt, that is, in the world.

(5) Viewing His People as Sheaves of Life
and as the Sun, the Moon, and the Stars of Light

(a) As Sheaves of Life

Now I have a heavy burden to share something very meaningful with you. If you had been Joseph, would you have considered your brothers heavenly and full of life and light? In 37:2 we are told that Joseph brought to his father an evil report regarding his brothers. Furthermore, according to chapter thirty-seven, Joseph's brothers were full of hatred and anger, and according to chapter thirty-eight, they were full of lust. In chapter thirty-seven we see the hatred and anger of Joseph's brothers, and in chapter thirty-eight we see Judah's lust. Joseph saw the evil of his brothers and reported it to his father. But Joseph had two dreams (37:5-9). In the first dream Joseph saw sheaves in the field. This dream reveals that, at the most, Joseph was just a sheaf and that, at the worst, his brothers also were sheaves. God gave Joseph this dream, and in it he had God's view of his brothers. Joseph might have said to his father, "Daddy, my brothers are so poor. How I have suffered from their evil! Oh, they are full of anger and lust!" But God came to give Joseph a dream, and He seemed to say, "Joseph, in My eyes you are the same as your brothers, and they are just as good as you are. You are a sheaf, and they also are sheaves. The only difference between you and them is that I have chosen you to reign. But this does not mean that you are better than they are."

If we do not have experience, we shall not be able to understand the word in the Bible regarding Joseph's dream of the sheaves. When you first come into the church life, you may say, "How wonderful the church life is! The brothers and sisters are all marvelous! How I love the church!" However, the more you love the church and care for the saints, the more "gophers," "turtles," and "scorpions" you will see. Then you will say, "Lord, what is this? Lord, the situation in the church is pitiful. Not even the elders are any good. And look at all the sisters! I don't want to sit near them in the meetings." At such a time you need a heavenly dream. When the dream comes, the Lord will tell you, "You are not any better, and the others are not worse than you. You are all sheaves of life in Me. There are no 'gophers,' 'scorpions,' or 'turtles' among My people. All are sheaves full of life." If I had not seen such a heavenly dream, I would have quit long ago. But I have seen the dream. I have seen that I am a sheaf and that all those who in my eyes are "gophers" are sheaves also. In the eyes of God, they are sheaves.

Years ago, I prayed many accusing prayers to the Lord; I reported to Him the evils I had seen. In my prayers I said, "Lord, I have given up my job and consecrated my life and my future for this work. But, Lord, look at this people!" Eventually, however, the dream came, and the Lord said to me, "You are not better than they. At the most, you are just a sheaf, and, at the worst, they also are sheaves." At the beginning I was troubled and argued with the Lord, saying, "Lord, You are not thorough. You are superficial. Don't You see their heart?" But the Lord said, "I don't look at them from your view. I see them from My view. In the New Jerusalem there are no 'gophers' and 'scorpions.'"

One day I received great help by reading Balaam's prophecy in Numbers 23. According to the book of Numbers, the children of Israel had done many evil things. Balaam was hired by a heathen king to curse Israel and to expose the evil in Israel. But God spoke through Balaam, and Balaam said, "He hath not beheld iniquity in Jacob, neither hath he seen perverseness in Israel" (Num. 23:21). God seemed to be saying, "I have not beheld any iniquity in My people. I do not see any perverseness in them."

Elijah complained against Israel saying, "The children of Israel have forsaken thy covenant, thrown down thine altars, and slain thy prophets with the sword; and I, even I only, am left; and they seek my life, to take it away" (1 Kings 19:10). Elijah was accusing Israel before God. Being displeased with this, the Lord replied, "Yet I have left me seven thousand in Israel, all the knees which have not bowed unto Baal, and every mouth which hath not kissed him" (1 Kings 19:18). Do not go to the Lord in the way of accusing others before Him. Instead, you should say to Him, "Lord, since You see no iniquity, I do not choose to see any either. All the 'gophers' and 'scorpions' are sheaves, and I love them."

However, this is not easy to do. You may even think that I am teaching you to lie, for you may say, "Brother So-and-so is pitiful. I could never say that he is a sheaf." But who is right—God or you? And what about the dream? If you have seen the heavenly dream, then you have seen that in God's view all His people are sheaves full of life to produce food for the meal offering to satisfy God and man.

(b) As the Sun, the Moon, and the Stars of Light

In the Bible there is the principle of confirmation by two witnesses. Thus, Joseph had two dreams. In Joseph's second dream he saw the sun, the moon, and the eleven stars bowing down to him (37:9). This indicates that in the eyes of God all the condemned and accused people are full of light. Be careful not to accuse the brothers and sisters. The reigning aspect of the maturity of life never condemns others. Rather, it shepherds and appreciates them. It says, "Oh, the church life and all the saints are wonderful! The saints are sheaves full of life. How nourishing and satisfying they are! Furthermore, they are heavenly luminaries full of light." If you say that it is a lie to speak this way and that you cannot do it, it means that you have not seen the dream, the vision. You are lacking the heavenly view.

Let me address this question to those who have been in the church life a long time: Do you still feel that the church is so good and that all the saints are wonderful? If you are honest, you will admit that you have criticized certain saints to your wife or husband. Perhaps some years ago you felt positively about all the brothers and sisters, but not today. Years ago, according to your natural view, all the saints were so good. But today you need the view of the heavenly dream. In Genesis 37 there are two dreams. One is of sheaves full of life, and the other of the heavenly host full of light. This is God's view, the heavenly view, of His people. Because I have this heavenly view, I am greatly encouraged. I am not working with "gophers" and "scorpions." I am serving the sheaves, I am under the sun and moon, and I am walking among the stars. The dream Joseph saw is similar to the vision in Revelation 12, where God's people are signified by the woman clothed with the sun, with the moon under her feet, and with the crown of twelve stars upon her head. We need such a vision to see God's people from the heavenly viewpoint.

One thing is certain: Whoever condemns the church or blames the saints will suffer the loss of life. There is not one exception to this. You may be right, and the church may actually be wrong. The condition of the saints may be that of "gophers" and "scorpions." But if you condemn them, you will suffer the loss of life. However, if you say, "Lord, I praise You because Your people are full of life and light," you will be the first to participate in life. For this reason, I dare not say that the brothers and sisters are not good. Rather, I always say, "Praise the Lord! How good the saints are!" When I do this, I enjoy life. But if I were to criticize the brothers and sisters,

I would immediately suffer death. No one who speaks negatively concerning the church or the saints enjoys life. On the contrary, all those who speak negatively suffer death. We need to say, "Praise the Lord, my brother will be a heavenly light! If he is not so today, he will be in the future." With God there is no time element. There is no clock in heaven, only eternity. As God views His people from the standpoint of eternity, He sees them all as sheaves full of life and as the sun, moon, and stars full of light.

(c) Positioned in Heaven, but Living on Earth

Although God's people are positioned in heaven as the sun, the moon, and the stars, they are living on earth as sheaves (Phil. 3:20; 2:15), for sheaves grow in the field. Today we are the heavenly people living on earth.

We are God's people. I have been encouraged, strengthened, and edified by this. I have complete faith in you all, and I expect to see you all in the New Jerusalem. I like to have an eternal view, not the view from the earth. I do not want to view things according to my limited sight. Rather, I would use the divine telescope. If you say that the brothers and sisters are so bad, it means that you are extremely shortsighted. But if you use the divine telescope to see through time, you will behold the New Jerusalem where there is nothing but sheaves and stars. In the New Jerusalem there are no "gophers" or "scorpions." There, everything is full of life and light. When we consider Joseph's dreams, we realize that no human mind could have conceived the book of Genesis. Only God could have caused Joseph to have these dreams.

(d) Actually Being Sinful

Although Joseph saw these two dreams, he still suffered the hatred and conspiracy of his brothers in that very chapter. Furthermore, in the following chapter we see Judah's lust. This indicates that actually the sons of Jacob were evil. Nevertheless, in the heavenly view they were not evil; they were sheaves full of life and stars full of light. The reason these two chapters are put together is so that we may have a contrast. In God's view the sons of Jacob are bright, but actually they are dark. In actuality they were sinful. Now we can understand why chapter thirty-eight follows chapter thirty-seven.

(e) Christ Still Coming through Them

Although the sons of Jacob were sinful, Christ still came through them (38:27-30; Matt. 1:3). Out of the gross sin committed in chapter thirty-eight, two sons were born, the first of whom was a forefather of Christ. Pharez, mentioned in the genealogy of Christ in Matthew 1, was one of Christ's forefathers. According to the holy word of Scripture, Christ came through the sinful sons of Jacob. It is similar to David's sin with Bathsheba. The issue of that sin was Solomon, who was also a forefather of Christ, one through whom Christ came (Matt. 1:6).

Do not believe that the church is not good, and do not complain against the saints or say that they are "scorpions." Out of a seemingly hopeless church, full of saints who, in your eyes, are "scorpions," Christ will come forth. However, this does not mean that we should do evil that good may come. Rather, it is a testimony of God's sovereign grace. Whether the believers are good or bad, we must be careful not to speak against them. If we do, God will say, "I do not see any iniquity or perverseness among them. My Christ will come through them. Don't you condemn them." We all need such a heavenly vision.

The mature life has a reigning aspect. The more mature in life you become, the less you will speak negatively concerning the saints or the church. When we came into the church, we had a church-life honeymoon. The honeymoon, however, never lasts very long. After your church-life honeymoon has ended, you may say, "I thought the church would be so good. But actually it is not good at all. If I could find something better, I would certainly not stay here. But, sorry to say, I cannot find anything better. However, I'm still looking. I may even go somewhere to start something on my own. Regardless of what I do, the church here is certainly not very good." Whenever you speak like this, you will suffer death. But one day the heavenly dream will come, and your view will be revolutionized. You will realize that you dare not say anything negative concerning the church or the saints. On the contrary, you will say, "This is the church, and this is God's people. In God's eyes the believers are all sheaves. They are also the sun, the moon, and the stars." When you come to this stage, you will not dare to say anything negative about the church.

After seeing such a vision, I have nevertheless said at times, "Yes, I have seen that the church is wonderful. But actually it is not so." In saying this, the "tail" was exposed. Even this "tail" caused me to suffer death. Eventually, I was completely subdued and convinced, and I said, "Lord, I forget my short sight and use the divine telescope. The church is excellent, marvelous, and wonderful. There is nothing wrong with the church. It is perfect and complete." When I speak like this, I am full of life and I enjoy life. To me, every brother and sister is wonderful, and I love them all, including the backsliders. The more I speak this way about the brothers and sisters, the more I am full of life. I believe many of us have experienced this. We are not the ones to judge. God is the Judge. And He is not judging the saints; He is working on them to transform the "scorpions" into sheaves and the "gophers" into stars. Eventually, we all shall be sheaves and stars. May we all have this eternal view.

(6) His People to Be under His Reign

Eventually, all Joseph's people will be under his reign (37:8). Joseph signifies the reigning aspect of the mature life. Only the mature life can reign, just as Christ reigns over the Jews (Matt. 27:11; John 19:19).

LIFE-STUDY OF GENESIS

MESSAGE ONE HUNDRED ELEVEN

JOSEPH'S LIVING CORRESPONDING WITH HIS VISION

The book of Genesis, in which nearly all of the truths in the Bible are sown as seeds, may be considered a biography of eight great men: Adam, Abel, Enoch, Noah, Abraham, Isaac, Jacob, and Joseph. These eight men are arranged in two groups of four. Adam, Abel, Enoch, and Noah make up the first group; and Abraham, Isaac, Jacob, and Joseph form the second. The first group represents the created race, the Adamic race, whereas the second group represents the called race, the Abrahamic race. Because of the failure of the created race, God had a new start with the called race. The created race began with Adam and ended with Noah. At both the beginning and the ending, the created race was a failure. Adam, the head of God's created race and its representative, became fallen. With Abel we have the coming back to God. In Adam, man fell away from God; but through God's redemption, Abel came back to Him. Enoch, who came after Abel, not only returned to God, but also walked with God. The issue of his life was a type of the rapture. Enoch was raptured out of death unto God. Enoch's life issued in Noah, who also walked with God and who had an experience of reigning, although his reigning was neither adequate nor full. However, Noah's reigning issued in a fall. Noah's descendants rebelled against God at Babel, and that rebellion resulted in God's giving up of the created race. Forced to have a new beginning, God visited Abraham and called him out of the rebellious created race. This marked the beginning of a new race, the called race, the Abrahamic race.

With this called race God certainly achieved a great success. Beginning with Abraham and continuing through Isaac and Jacob, the way rose higher and higher. Eventually we see a full reign in Jacob. As we have pointed out, Abraham, Isaac, Jacob, and Joseph should not be considered separate individuals. Rather, they represent four aspects of a complete, mature saint. In them we see God's selection, God's calling, and justification by faith. We see how a called and justified saint can live in the presence of God by faith to enjoy all the riches of the inheritance. However, such a one still strives to gain the birthright. But all his struggles cause him nothing but suffering. In his sufferings God's hand comes upon him to deal with him, and he is dealt with by God until he becomes mature. Hallelujah, in the called race we see the maturity of life! This matured life has a reigning aspect, an aspect portrayed by the life of Joseph. This is the reason that in the book of Genesis Joseph is so excellent and marvelous.

When I was young, my mother used to tell us Bible stories. She spent a long time on the story of Joseph. Oh, how I sympathized with this excellent one when I heard that he was cast into a pit and sold into slavery! Although I loved Joseph and realized that he was someone special, I did not know why he was so excellent. I knew only that Joseph was very good and that I wanted to be like him. Even after I had ministered the Word for years, I still did not know the reason for Joseph's excellence. But now I can boldly give you the reason Joseph was excellent: it was because he was the reigning aspect of the mature life. And he was the reigning aspect of a matured Israel, not of Jacob. Thus, Joseph was the cream of a matured life.

What we see in Joseph, of course, is simply a shadow. In reality and in actuality, the reigning aspect typified by Joseph is Christ constituted into our being. We all are Jacobs, but we have the constitution of Christ within us. On the day we were regenerated, Christ was constituted into us. Eventually this Christ becomes our constitution. That part of our being that is constituted with Christ is neither our flesh nor our mind; rather, it is our spirit. Second Timothy 4:22 says that Christ is with our spirit. This means that Christ is constituted into the depths of our being. The Christ-constituted aspect of our regenerated being is fully represented, portrayed, and typified by Joseph. Because Joseph represents the reigning aspect of a victorious and mature life, his life is recorded in the Bible in such an excellent way.

I. LIVING AS A SHEAF OF LIFE

The first three chapters regarding the reigning part of a matured life are chapters thirty-seven, thirty-eight, and thirty-nine. As a child, I used to dislike these chapters because they were filled with hatred, plotting, and betrayals. Chapter thirty-eight is a record of Judah's incest, and in chapter thirty-nine we see darkness and the indulgence in lust. Have you ever loved these chapters? After I was saved and began to love the Bible, I did not spend much time on these chapters. Having become familiar with the story found in them, I did not care to read these chapters again. When in 1955 I conducted a study on the book of Genesis, I skipped over them. But during the twenty-three years since that study was conducted, I have received more light. After I came to this country, I saw the value, the preciousness, of Joseph's dreams, which are the controlling view of these chapters. If you have not seen the vision of Joseph's dreams, you will be able to know no more than the story contained in these chapters. You will not be able to know the depths of the significance of this story. Joseph's dreams controlled and directed his life. Joseph conducted himself in such an excellent way as the reigning aspect of a mature life under the direction of this controlling vision.

Chapter thirty-seven begins by telling us how Jacob loved his dear son Joseph, and how Joseph reported the evils of his brothers to his father. Then we are told about Joseph's dreams (37:5-10). In these days the Lord has shown us that Joseph's dreams reveal the actual situation of God's people in His eyes. God's people are all sheaves of life. A sheaf is a bundle of wheat full of life and life supply. The sheaves contain life grains which are good for life supply. Do not say, "I don't like the Israelites, because they are so evil." Remember the case of the Gentile prophet Balaam who was bribed to pronounce a curse upon Israel. At that time, Israel actually was evil. Nevertheless, Balaam, under the control of God, said that God had not beheld iniquity in Jacob nor perverseness in

Israel (Num. 23:21). On the contrary, in God's eyes all His chosen people are sheaves of life, full of life supply. Furthermore, God's people are like stars shining in the sky.

After telling us of these two dreams, the record of the book of Genesis reveals that Joseph's brothers plotted to kill him and that he was sold into slavery in Egypt. In chapter thirty-eight we see the incestuous sin of Judah, and in chapter thirty-nine, the darkest temptation and most unjust treatment of Joseph. According to the sequence of events in these chapters, we see that Joseph's excellent behavior was under the direction of his dreams. In his first dream he saw that he was one of the sheaves; and he was not a sheaf falling down, but a sheaf rising up. I believe that from the time of that dream Joseph realized where God had put him and what God wanted him to be. He no doubt understood that God wanted him to be such a sheaf. He was not to be driftwood full of death, but a sheaf standing up full of life. If you had had such a dream, would you not be influenced, if not controlled, by it? Would this dream not govern your behavior and direct your conduct? Certainly it would. I believe that Joseph's dream of the sheaf directed his behavior.

This was also true of the second dream, the dream of the sun, the moon, and twelve stars. Suppose you had a dream in which you were the star that was worshipped by the other stars. Would you not as a result esteem yourself highly? Would you not say, "My, I am a star! I am not a scorpion or something low and dark. I am a bright star shining in the heavens." If you had been the one to see such a vision, would it not control you? If it did not control you for the rest of your life, it would at least govern you for a period of time. You would begin to behave like a shining star and say, "Last night I saw that I was the star worshipped by all the other stars. From now on, I must act like such a bright star. In the past I have been dark, but I must not be like this any longer. Instead, I must be bright and shining."

Joseph behaved so excellently and marvelously because he was directed by the vision he saw in his dreams. Children are influenced by what they see on television. I have observed my own grandchildren act out what they saw on a certain program. If even the little ones are influenced by what they see, then how much more was the young man Joseph influenced by the heavenly vision, the vision that he was a sheaf rising up full of life and that he was a star worshipped by all the other stars! Do you not believe that Joseph was influenced and impressed by this vision? I definitely believe that he was. The point I am making is that Joseph's excellent and marvelous behavior was due to the vision he received. The vision of his two dreams controlled his life and directed his behavior. He behaved as the sheaf standing up and full of life, and he conducted himself like a heavenly star shining in the darkness. With this viewpoint, you are able to understand the significance of these three chapters.

A. His Brothers Giving Vent to Their Anger

In these chapters two gross sins are recorded. In chapter thirty-seven there is the sin of anger (37:18-28). Joseph's brothers seized the opportunity to give full vent to their anger. This was not an insignificant case of anger. The one Joseph's brothers were plotting to kill was not a thief, but their own brother in the flesh, the dear son of their own father. If they had had any human affection at all, they would never have considered doing such a thing. Reuben, however, did think of how it would affect their father; and Judah suggested that they not kill him, but sell him, which was far superior to shedding his blood. Nevertheless, in chapter thirty-seven we see the anger of Joseph's brothers. In the next chapter, chapter thirty-eight, we have Judah's indulgence in lust, even in incest (38:15-18). After the fall of man, the first issue to come forth was the killing of a brother in the flesh. And the sin that brought in the flood as God's judgment upon the fallen race was the indulgence in lust. These two sins, the sins of murdering a brother in the flesh and of indulging in lust, are repeated here.

B. Joseph Emerging from Anger, Surviving in a Death Situation

The anger of his brothers afforded Joseph the opportunity to live as a sheaf of life. While all his brothers were drowning in the water of anger, Joseph, the reigning aspect of the mature life, lived as a sheaf of life, emerging from the death water of human anger. The record, under God's inspiration, uses fallen anger as the background to demonstrate how much life was in the sheaf. This sheaf was filled with life. When all the rest had sunk into the death water of human anger, this sheaf emerged and survived in that situation of death.

Is this not also the record of our life? Day after day, we are surrounded by the death water of human anger. But instead of drowning, we emerge out of the death water and survive. If this is a portrait of your daily life, then you are the reigning aspect of the victorious life. Although, humanly speaking, we are prone to lose our temper, we nonetheless have the constitution of Christ that emerges out of the situation of anger. Thus, we are today's Josephs, sheaves of life rising up and standing up.

II. LIVING AS A STAR OF LIGHT

A. His Brother Judah Indulging in Lust

The second gross sin, the indulgence in lust, also afforded Joseph an opportunity. The indulgence in lust seen in chapter thirty-eight is a symbol of darkness. In this chapter Judah was utterly in darkness. Judah behaved in a blind way, and blindness signifies darkness. If he had not been in blindness, in darkness, how could he have committed adultery with his daughter-in-law? Where was his conscience? Where was his eyesight? His eyes had been blackened and blinded, and he was in darkness. That evil woman in chapter thirty-nine, the wife of Potiphar, was also in darkness. If she had not been in darkness, how could she have behaved in such an evil way? Thus, in chapters thirty-eight and thirty-nine we have a portrait of darkness.

B. Joseph Overcoming Lust, Shining in Darkness

But in the midst of this darkness we see Joseph as a bright star shining in the heavens (39:7-12). Conducting himself as a shining star, Joseph seemed to be saying, "All you people are under darkness, but I am shining upon you. How can I, a bright star, do such a dark thing? I cannot forget my dream. My dream controls me and directs me. As a heavenly star, I would never sell my position." If you have this light as you come to these chapters, you will see that Joseph was one who lived a life that corresponded to his vision. Joseph was not only a dreamer; he was also one who practiced, one who lived out, what he saw in his dream.

As today's Josephs, we also must have some dreams. Others should say that we are dreamers. Many of my Christian friends consider me a dreamer. In talking about the overcoming life and the practice of the church life, they have said to me, "Brother Lee, these are wonderful ideas, but they are just dreams. No one can live such a victorious life on this earth, and it is impossible to have the practice of the church life. We must wait for that day. Let's not dream any more. Rather, let's wake up from the dreams." But I not only have dreams—I practice what I see in my dreams. You may think that I am merely a dreamer, but I am also one who fully puts my dreams into practice. I can testify that it is very possible to have an overcoming life and to have the practical church life. This is not simply my dream; it is my practice and my experience. Like Joseph, I have had some dreams, the dream of the sheaves and of the bright stars. By the Lord's mercy, I have lived according to my dreams. I have behaved and conducted myself according to the vision I have seen. Although some say, "These are merely dreams without any possibility of fulfillment," I must declare that these are heavenly revelations of the facts. Do you not believe that the victorious life is entirely possible? And do you not believe that the practical church life is available today? We are not dreaming in vain. We have a vision that controls us.

We all know what it is to lose our temper. I am no exception. It is not a good thing to keep our temper within us. On the contrary, in a sense we feel better when we give vent to it. However, when I am about to lose my temper, the vision of the sheaf comes, and the Lord asks me, "Are you a sheaf rising up? If you are, then what about your temper?" As soon as the Lord speaks to me in this way and I respond to Him, my anger is gone. Even if I wanted to lose my temper, I would not be able to do so. It is possible for us all to live without anger and loss of temper. As you are about to lose your temper, the Lord may say, "Are you a sheaf? Are you one in the church, in the Lord's recovery?" As soon as you say that you are a sheaf, your anger will vanish.

Just as we all have anger, we also have lust. If you have no lust, then you must be a bench or a stone. Every human being has lust. The way to control our lust is to be subdued, controlled, and directed by the vision. Oh, we have a vision controlling us! The people perish when they do not have a vision. Because we have seen the vision, it is very difficult for us to indulge in lust.

The function of the vision is similar to that of brakes in a car. In times of danger, we step on the brakes. The vision of the heavenly star is a powerful brake for our spiritual car. We are not driving a car that is without controls. When we are driving properly in the right lane, there is no need to use the brakes. But when the car begins to go out of control, the brakes work immediately. Hallelujah for such a controlling vision! Many of us can testify that before we came into the church life, we were like a car without brakes. But after coming into the church life, we saw the controlling vision, and powerful brakes were installed in our car. Here in the church life we have the vision of the sheaf and the vision of the star.

III. LIVING THE KINGDOM LIFE

Joseph's life under the heavenly vision was the life of the kingdom of the heavens described in Matthew 5, 6, and 7. According to the constitution of the heavenly kingdom revealed in these chapters in Matthew, our anger must be subdued and our lust conquered (Matt. 5:21-32). If we claim to be the kingdom people, yet we cannot subdue our anger or conquer our lust, we are finished. Instead of being in the kingdom, we are on the seashore. We are those giving vent to our anger and indulging in lust. But all the kingdom people subdue their anger and conquer their lust. This is the kingdom life.

In the kingdom life today, kings are being trained. We, the

kingdom people in the kingdom life, are being trained to be kings, to be Josephs, to be the reigning aspect of the mature life. For this, we must subdue our anger and conquer our lust. What a wonderful picture Joseph's life is of our experience today! Day by day, we are subduing our anger and conquering our lust. Instead of agreeing with our anger or cooperating with our lust, we reject our anger and condemn our lust, because we are the reigning aspect of the mature life. We have the constitution of Christ within us, and we are being prepared to reign as kings.

IV. ENJOYING THE LORD'S PRESENCE

A life such as Joseph's always has the presence of the Lord (39:2-5, 21-23). Wherever the presence of the Lord is, there is authority. If you have the presence of the Lord, the authority of the Lord will be with you. For example, in captivity Daniel had the Lord's presence; therefore, the Lord's authority was with him. Even a child in a family may have the Lord's presence and therefore be the genuine authority in that family. In the case of Joseph, Potiphar, an officer in Pharaoh's palace, was in control of things. Eventually, however, Potiphar was under Joseph's control because Joseph had the Lord's presence. Also consider Joseph's experience in prison. Although there was a ruler over the prison, eventually this ruler was not the actual ruler. Instead, Joseph, a prisoner who had the presence of God, became the ruler. Both in Potiphar's house and in the prison Joseph became king.

Wherever the constitution of Christ goes with the presence of God, there will be the reigning part. In the coming kingdom it will be this part that will be the co-kings with Christ in the kingdom of the heavens. Thus, the reigning aspect of the mature life is a life that always enjoys the presence of the Lord. The authority in this universe is the Lord Himself. Wherever His presence is, there is authority, the ruling power. As long as we have the Lord's presence, we have authority, even if we are in prison. Although we may be prisoners, we shall eventually become rulers. We shall rule wherever we are. This indicates that we are the reigning aspect of the mature life.

A. Prospered by the Lord

In the presence of the Lord, Joseph was prospered by Him (39:2-3, 23). Where the presence of the Lord is, there is not only the Lord's authority, but also prosperity brought about by the Lord's sovereignty. While Joseph was undergoing ill-treatment, he enjoyed the prosperity that came to him under the Lord's sovereignty.

B. The Favor with the Lord's Blessing

In the Lord's presence, Joseph was favored with the Lord's blessing wherever he was. The Lord's blessing always accompanies prosperity under His sovereignty. When Joseph enjoyed prosperity, he and those who were involved with him were blessed (39:4-5, 22-23).

LIFE-STUDY OF GENESIS

MESSAGE ONE HUNDRED TWELVE

BEING MATURED
THE REIGNING ASPECT OF THE MATURED ISRAEL

(2)

In the book of Genesis, Joseph represents the reigning aspect of the mature life. As such a representative, Joseph typifies Christ, for the reigning aspect of the mature life is Christ constituted into our being. Therefore, in the record of Genesis Joseph typifies Christ.

(7) Betrayed

We have seen that Joseph typifies Christ as the beloved Son of God, as the One sent by God the Father to shepherd God's people, and as the One who was persecuted by those whom He was sent to shepherd. In addition, according to the four Gospels, Christ was betrayed (Matt. 26:14-16). Joseph, as a type of Christ, also was betrayed (Gen. 37:27-28). In the biblical sense, to be betrayed means to be despised, depreciated, dishonored, or disregarded. When Judas was about to sell Christ, he certainly was lowering down the value of Christ to the uttermost. In Matthew 26 we see that Christ was a test to all those around Him. Some hated Him. Mary, however, appreciated Him and poured valuable ointment upon Him. To Mary, Christ was valuable, and she highly appreciated Him. But Judas despised Christ, dishonored Him, and disregarded Him. He depreciated Christ to such a degree that he sold Him for a cheap price, for thirty pieces of silver, which according to Exodus was the price of a slave (Exo. 21:32). Thus, in the Bible to betray someone means to depreciate him.

Whenever you are depreciated by someone, it means that you are betrayed by him. Whenever your wife depreciates you, she is betraying you. Likewise, if the brothers disregard you, it means that you have been betrayed. Consider how you evaluate yourself. In your thinking are you not valuable? We all regard ourselves as valuable. Therefore, when we are depreciated by others or disregarded by them, we are betrayed. You may think that during the years you have been in the church life you have never seen a betrayal. However, in the church life people are often betrayed in the sense of being disregarded or depreciated. Day after day, husbands may depreciate their wives or wives may disregard their husbands. If some saints talk about another saint in a depreciating way, they are betraying him.

We all think of ourselves as valuable. In actuality we are valuable because we have Christ in us. Do you not have God within you? In the Bible God is likened to gold, and Christ is likened to a treasure. Our God is the gold within us, and Christ within us is the treasure in the vessel. The unbelievers do not have such a high value because they do not have Christ within them. At most, they are simply muddy vessels. But we have the greatest treasure within us. Therefore, we should not think that we are not valuable. We need to declare to the angels, "Angels, you must realize how valuable I am. I'm valuable because Christ is in me." Furthermore, you may boast to Satan and to the demons, "Satan, I want you to know that I have God and Christ within me. Demons, you are not destined to have Christ in you. But I have Christ in me and therefore I am valuable." This is not pride; on the contrary, it is true humility. I would like to tell everyone, including the angels, the Devil, the demons, and everyone on earth, that I am valuable because I have Christ; therefore, you must not despise me or disregard me.

We must learn not to sell our brothers. Joseph was sold by his brothers. If they had regarded him as a sheaf or a star, they would not have sold him. The fact that they betrayed Joseph means that they depreciated him and disregarded him. In principle, the same thing happened to the Lord Jesus. Although He was precious and valuable, Judas depreciated Him and sold Him for thirty pieces of silver. Peter, James, John, and all the other Apostles followed the footsteps of the Lamb, and they also were depreciated. This was also true of the Apostle Paul. Throughout the centuries, the followers of the Lamb have been betrayed. Like Christ, they have been depreciated, disregarded, and despised. As we follow the Lord today, we also are being depreciated. We endure many sufferings simply because we are despised and disregarded. Those who oppose us depreciate us and disregard us. If they appreciated the treasure within us and recognized the preciousness of what the Lord has wrought into us, they would neither despise us nor disregard us. Certain ones oppose us because they depreciate us. This depreciation is actually a form of selling us, and it is a sign of betrayal. Do not think that such a betrayal happened only to Joseph or to Christ as typified by Joseph. On the contrary, it has happened to all the followers of Christ and it is our experience today.

Before we were saved, many of us were highly regarded by our parents, relatives, and friends. But after we were saved and began to seek the Lord, our friends, relatives, and in some cases even our parents began to despise us. This is betrayal. Christ's crucifixion began with His betrayal. He was crucified after He was betrayed. It was the same in principle with Joseph. He was not directly cast into prison. First he was sold, and his being sold was the stepping-stone into prison. Christ's betrayal was the stepping-stone to the cross. It is not an insignificant matter to be betrayed. All the persecution and opposition today is a type of betrayal. Those who oppose us are betraying us; they are selling us at a cheap price. Although we are valuable, the opposers sell us for such a low price, even for nothing.

(8) Delivered into the Prison of Death

Joseph's betrayal was followed by a period of confinement, a period of imprisonment (39:20). Joseph was with two criminals, who typified the two criminals with Christ, one of whom was restored and the other executed (40:1-23). It was the same with Christ. After Christ was betrayed, He was put into the prison of death (Acts 2:23). He was crucified between two criminals, one of whom was saved and the other perished (Luke 23:32, 39-43). Christ was confined in the prison of death for three days and three nights. As a type of Christ, Joseph had the same experience as Christ. He was rejected by his brothers, sold by them, and eventually cast into prison. Christ suffered the same things. Firstly, He was rejected by His brothers; then He was sold by one of His people, and eventually He was cast into the prison of death.

Although Christ was resurrected after His death, His resurrection did not come immediately afterward. Humanly speaking, the three days of Christ's confinement in the prison of death were not a short time. No night has ever lasted for three days and three nights. At the longest, night lasts from evening until morning. But the night Christ spent in the prison of death lasted for three days and three nights. If we had been Mary Magdalene, it would have been a long time to us, because she loved Christ, had followed Him, and had seen Him crucified and buried. After Christ's death and burial, Mary had no heart to eat or sleep. Instead, she waited for something to happen. I do not believe that all the disciples could have forgotten that before His death Christ had said that He would be resurrected after three days. Even if they were not clear about what He had said, they must have been impressed with something regarding His resurrection. This must have been especially true of the sisters, for they often have a better memory than the brothers. Although Peter might not have been impressed with Christ's coming resurrection, I do not believe that Mary Magdalene forgot that Jesus said that after three days He would rise from the dead. It was very difficult for her to wait for those three days. It would have been difficult to wait even three hours. At last, on the third day, the tomb where Jesus was buried was found empty. The three days and nights that Christ had been confined in the prison of death were a long night. Joseph's night of confinement lasted approximately ten years. When Joseph was sold into slavery in Egypt, he was about seventeen years of age; and when he was released from prison, he was thirty. If you read the Bible carefully, you will see that it was not long after Joseph was sold to Potiphar that he was cast into prison. Joseph, therefore, was in prison for a long period of time, a long time of darkness.

According to the Bible, it is the young people, not the older ones, who experience this lesson. When Joseph was put into prison, he was less than twenty years old. Every young person needs such a period of confinement. Young people, because you are so free, you need to be confined. In this country the young people are eager to be eighteen years of age, for then they can be free like birds released from a cage. I have observed this with my own grandchildren. At the age of eighteen, they think they can be released from the cage. However, if the young people love the Lord and are today's Joseph, they will be placed into the Lord's confinement after they have been released from their cage. Young people, the Lord's confinement is awaiting you.

We have seen that Joseph represents the reigning aspect of the mature life. However, before Joseph was enthroned and came into power, he was imprisoned. This indicates that before enthronement, there is confinement. In Joseph's dreams, there was no indication that he would be imprisoned. The dreams must have made Joseph very happy. In them he saw himself as a standing sheaf and as a shining star. Joseph was so excited about his dreams that he told his brothers about them, not realizing that they would be offended by them. Enthronement did not immediately follow Joseph's dreams. Instead, there was betrayal leading to imprisonment.

After hearing this, some of you may say, "The previous messages on Joseph were wonderful and glorious, but I can't take this word. I quit." But even if you quit, God will not quit. You need to realize that you are a kite on a string, and that string is in the Lord's hand. The Lord would say, "Do you intend to give up? I will not allow you to give up."

If Joseph had not had those dreams, he probably would not have been in any trouble. But he had two dreams and in his excitement told his brothers about them. Joseph, however, was not immediately enthroned. Instead, he was depreciated and imprisoned. Some of the young people may think that if they follow Jesus Christ and are in the Lord's recovery, everything will be glorious. However, the young people need a period of confinement. This is very important for them. How I thank the Lord for what confinement has done for me!

Your prison may be your wife. Many of you young people were not married when you came into the church life. In the church you had the opportunity to make the best selection. However, after the honeymoon, you found that your dear wife became your confinement. You may say, "What has happened? Now that I am married I am no longer free." That is correct. Your husband or wife is your prison. Every marriage and every home is a prison. Thank the Lord for all these prisons. As many of us can testify, this confinement lasts a long time. I have been in this type of prison for a great many years, and because I still need confinement, I am still in prison. I still have some lessons to learn.

Now we come to my burden in this message: I want to share with you, as a parenthetical word, the secret of how to spend your time during your imprisonment. This is the secret of enjoying your imprisonment. Without this secret, I could not understand Genesis 40 in a full way. Now I would like to present to you the secret of what we should do during our period of imprisonment. When the time comes for you to be imprisoned, you will understand that what I am presenting to you in this message is altogether workable.

I. JOSEPH TRIED BY HIS DREAMS
NOT BEING FULFILLED

Joseph was tested by the fact that his dreams were not fulfilled. Immediately after Joseph had his dreams, he told his parents and brothers about them. Not long after that, he was sold into slavery and then cast into prison where, I believe, he stayed over ten years. In his dreams there was no indication or implication that Joseph would suffer. However, immediately after Joseph had those dreams, he had to endure suffering. Likewise, I can testify that the throne does not immediately follow the vision of Christ, the church, the cross, or the inner life. Instead, there is suffering, trial, betrayal, and imprisonment. According to our natural concept, we think that immediately after we see a vision, something glorious will happen in our life. But this is not the case. After the vision, trials will come. Young people, do not think that after you have seen the vision of Christ, the church, the cross, the inner life, or the Spirit, you will have a glorious time. No, you will suffer and be imprisoned.

If I had been Joseph, I might have had doubts about my dreams and said to myself, "These dreams are not something real. I dreamed that I was a sheaf standing up, but actually I have been made low. I saw that I was a star shining in heaven, but actually I have been cast into the dungeon. What has happened is the exact opposite of my dreams." I would certainly have doubted my interpretation of my dreams. I would have regarded them as unreal.

Those of us who have been in the church life for many years have had this experience. Perhaps some years ago you saw a wonderful vision concerning Christ and the church life. Perhaps you even sang about the glorious church life. But what has actually happened in the church life has not been that excellent or glorious. Therefore, you might have said, "I thought I was in the good land of Canaan, but I actually was in Egypt. I dreamed that I was surrounded by sheaves, but actually I am surrounded by 'Egyptian scorpions.' According to the vision I saw and according to the messages Brother Lee gave us, I expected to be in the third heaven. But now I am in a dungeon, in a pit. Instead of being in Jerusalem, I am in Egypt." Many of us can testify of experiences like this. Following the vision there came, not enthronement, but imprisonment.

II. JOSEPH HAVING THE FAITH AND THE BOLDNESS TO INTERPRET THE DREAMS OF HIS TWO COMPANIONS IN PRISON

During his imprisonment, however, Joseph had the faith and the boldness to interpret the dreams of his two companions in prison even though his dreams were not yet fulfilled (40:8-19). It was just like Abraham praying for Abimelech to have children when God's promise to him about having a son had not yet been fulfilled (20:17-18). It is the same with us in the church life today. Some brothers and sisters are what we may call old-time dreamers. They are those who had dreams a long time ago. Although they were excited by the visions they saw and the wonderful messages they heard, they were later sold into Egypt. Instead of being surrounded by sheaves, they found themselves surrounded by "Egyptian scorpions"; and instead of being in the third heaven, they found themselves in prison. Then some latecomers joined them in prison, just as Joseph was joined in his confinement by the chief cupbearer and the baker. Joseph might have been in prison for nine or ten years already before he was joined by them. These latecomers also had some dreams. They could not understand their dreams, but Joseph was able to interpret them. Although Joseph's dreams had not yet been fulfilled, he had the faith and the boldness to interpret the dreams of his companions. If I had been Joseph, I would have said, "I interpreted my own dreams, but these interpretations have not been fulfilled. How can I have the boldness to give others the interpretation of their dreams? Even if I did know the meaning of their dreams, I would not have the assurance to tell them, because I don't know that my interpretations will be fulfilled." However, although Joseph's interpretation of his own dreams had not been fulfilled, he still had the boldness to say to his companions, "Do not interpretations belong to God? Tell me them, I pray you" (40:8). Joseph seemed to be saying, "I had two dreams, and God gave me the interpretation of them. I still believe in these interpretations, although they have not yet been fulfilled. I have the faith to interpret your dreams for you." Do you have the boldness to say that the church life is wonderful, even when you are surrounded by some "Egyptians"? Could you say this even when your dream of the church life has not yet been fulfilled and the church life is not wonderful to you? Joseph believed not only for himself, but also for others. It is easy to believe for others when your dreams have been fulfilled. If your dreams have been fulfilled according to your interpretation, it is easy to interpret the dreams of others. But in Joseph's case, even after a period of about ten years, the interpretation of his own dreams had not been fulfilled. It was difficult for one in such a situation to interpret the dreams of others. Nevertheless, Joseph did so.

    I have been engaged in the ministry of the Word for years. I saw certain visions in the early years and I interpreted what I saw. But even many years later the things that I saw and interpreted had not actually happened. When some latecomers needed my help, I wondered what to do. I wondered if I should say something like this: "I had some dreams many years ago, and I was given the interpretation of these dreams. But even until now my dreams have not been fulfilled. Therefore, I don't have the heart, the assurance, or the boldness to interpret your dreams for you. You should go talk to someone else." Joseph was not like this. Although his dreams had not yet been fulfilled, he still had the boldness and the assurance to interpret dreams for others. I can testify that I have done the same thing. I have encouraged others to go on according to the vision they saw, even though my visions had not been fulfilled. Certainly I was right in doing this. All the old-time dreamers must suffer something for the sake of the latecomers.

Andrew Murray once said a word like this: The good minister of the Word should always minister more than what he has experienced. This means that we should speak more according to the vision than according to the fulfillment of the vision. Even if our vision has not been fulfilled, we should still speak of it to others. The time will come when our vision will be fulfilled. Joseph's dreams were eventually fulfilled through his interpretation of the dream of the cupbearer.

III. JOSEPH CONFIRMED AND STRENGTHENED BY THE FULFILLMENT OF THE DREAMS OF HIS COMPANIONS IN PRISON

It was just a matter of days before the dreams of the cupbearer and the baker were fulfilled. When the dreams of Joseph's companions were fulfilled, Joseph was confirmed and strengthened. If I had been Joseph, I would certainly have been encouraged, and I would have said, "Even though I have not yet seen the fulfillment of my dreams, I have the confirmation that the fulfillment will certainly come. I interpreted the dreams of these two men, and the interpretations have come to pass. This will also happen in the case of my dreams. My fulfillment will also come."

IV. JOSEPH TRIED FURTHER BY HIS DREAMS NOT BEING FULFILLED FOR ANOTHER PERIOD OF TIME

The fulfillment of the dreams of Joseph's companions came in a few days. But Joseph was tried further by the fact that his dreams were not fulfilled for another period of time (40:14, 23). Genesis 41:1 indicates that another two full years went by. During these last two years, the test was most difficult. Before the cupbearer left the prison, Joseph pleaded with him to remember him, saying, "But remember me with thee when it shall be well with thee, and show kindness, I pray thee, unto me, and make mention of me unto Pharaoh, and bring me out of this house" (40:14, Heb.). Joseph seemed to be saying to the cupbearer, "When you are restored, remember me with you. Don't just remember yourself. When you are doing well and everything is going well with you, please remember me." Nevertheless, the chief cupbearer forgot Joseph (40:23). Joseph's dreams were confirmed, but they were still not fulfilled.

Before the confirmation of Joseph's dreams, Joseph had faith; and after the confirmation was given, he had more faith. The more faith we have, the more testing we shall suffer. Suppose you were Joseph there in confinement. What would you have said? Joseph might have said, "I had two dreams many years ago, and they have not been fulfilled. But these two men had a dream, and their dream was fulfilled after three days. How long will it be before my dreams are fulfilled?" Thus, the last two years were the most difficult period of Joseph's time of testing.

What we are describing in this message is not a mere doctrine. As we follow the heavenly vision, we shall trace Joseph's footsteps. Never think that Joseph was enthroned immediately after he saw the vision. No, he had to pass through a long period of trial and testing. The visions Joseph saw not only controlled his life; they also sustained his faith. This does not mean, however, that if your faith is stronger, the length of time until the fulfillment of your dreams will be shortened. Rather, the stronger your faith is, the longer the period of testing will be. Joseph's time of testing was much longer than that of his companions because he was more valuable than they. Because they were not so valuable, the time of their fulfillment came very quickly. Actually, for those two latecomers, there was nearly no testing. They each had a dream, and a few days later their dreams were fulfilled. Because Joseph was important and valuable, the time of his testing could not be shortened.

Young people, do not think that in just two years you will become a giant. No, like Joseph, you must wait until you are thirty years of age. The Bible is always consistent. For instance, the priests had to be thirty years old before they could enter into the full priesthood, and the Lord Jesus also began His ministry when He was thirty. Thus, in this matter also Joseph typified Christ. When he was thirty years of age, he was fully put into the ministry.

Some of you may think that this word about waiting until the age of thirty to be put into the full ministry is a contradiction of what I have said elsewhere regarding the elders of the church in Jerusalem probably being under the age of thirty. Yes, I did say that Peter, James, and John were probably between twenty-five and twenty-eight years of age when they became elders. However, we must pay attention to the principle, not to the literal figures regarding physical age. You may have a heart that is absolutely for the Lord, and you may have seen some visions. But do not think that you will be enthroned immediately. Instead, you must be prepared to be depreciated and confined. I am proud of the young brothers and sisters, many of whom are still teenagers. I am proud of the fact that they love the Lord so much and that they have seen certain things that most pastors have not seen. However, these young people must be ready not to be honored, but to be betrayed.

This was the experience of Brother Nee. Brother Nee was a very intelligent person. He was so keen in learning English and Chinese that his parents even hired a private teacher to instruct him in the Chinese classics. At the age of seventeen, he was saved and he began to love the Lord. Brother Nee wanted to attend a Bible school in Shanghai, founded for the training of young people by Dora Yu, the prevailing evangelist who had brought Brother Nee to the Lord. His mother, who also loved the Lord, agreed that he should go. Because both Brother Nee and his mother had been saved through the preaching of Dora Yu, they respected her very much. Although Brother Nee was an intelligent young man who eventually became the outstanding gift of this age to the church, he was rejected by Dora Yu, and after a period of time was sent home from Bible school. Brother Nee, who was very much seeking the Lord, was betrayed by the very one who had brought him to the Lord. Instead of appreciating his intelligence, Dora Yu depreciated him, misunderstood him, and rejected him. The reason he was sent home was an incident over an errand he was asked to take care of. It took him a longer time to take some mail from a suburb to the post office in downtown Shanghai than Dora Yu expected. Thinking that he was passing his time in amusement, Dora Yu sent him home to his mother. Thus, Brother Nee was rejected and misunderstood, that is, he was betrayed. However, Brother Nee was not discouraged. He left Shanghai, returned home, and went on to love the Lord all the more. He recognized that this experience was the Lord's dealing with him. Time after time, Brother Nee was betrayed.

Young people, be prepared for this. After you begin to seek the Lord, certain things will happen to you that seem unreasonable. Do not think that because you love the Lord and seek Him, everything will be glorious for you. No, sometimes you will be misunderstood, even by the brothers and sisters and the elders. Firstly you will be betrayed; then you will endure a period of confinement. We all need such confinement. Be assured, however, that wherever you will be, God's presence will be there with you.

Wherever you are, you will bring either life or death. To the cupbearer, Joseph brought life. In the cupbearer's dream we see a vine full of life. But to the baker, Joseph brought death, because the baker was devoured by birds. It is not an insignificant matter to be a Joseph, for wherever you go, people will either receive life or suffer death. Either they will go to Christ typified by the vine full of life, or they will be devoured by Satan, represented by the birds of the air. In

2 Corinthians 2:14 the Apostle Paul said, "But thanks be to God, who always leads us in triumph in the Christ, and manifests through us the savor of the knowledge of Him in every place." In verse 16 Paul says, "To the one a savor from death unto death, to the other a savor from life unto life." To the cupbearer, Joseph brought restoration. To the baker, Joseph brought execution. No matter who a person may be, if he contacts you, it will be either life or death to him. This is a very significant matter. This is the experience of Joseph.

Apparently as Joseph was in confinement, he was suffering. Actually, however, he was not suffering; he was learning valuable lessons and experiencing what was necessary for his enthronement. Without the lessons learned during confinement, how could Joseph, a young man, be enthroned in Egypt to rule over the whole country? It would have been impossible. Joseph was trained by his imprisonment. His confinement was truly an exercise for him. Young people, any confinement that you must undergo will be a training, an exercise, and a time of learning as a preparation for your enthronement. In order to come to the throne, you need to undergo the sufferings of betrayal and confinement. No one can skip over these sufferings. No ministry has ever been used by the Lord that has not passed through betrayal and imprisonment. Only by passing through betrayal and imprisonment shall we be qualified to ascend to the throne. After you have been trained through confinement, you will no longer be a youngster; rather, you will be a man qualified under God's training.

Do not think that Joseph was an exceptional case. No, Joseph's case is normal. You and I shall all be like him. Hallelujah for the vision! And hallelujah for the betrayal, for the confinement, and for all the lessons! Praise the Lord that we have the way to go on!

LIFE-STUDY OF GENESIS

MESSAGE ONE HUNDRED THIRTEEN

BEING MATURED
THE REIGNING ASPECT OF THE MATURED ISRAEL

(3)

In this message we come to Genesis 41, which unfolds more of the details of Joseph's life. As we have pointed out, Joseph represents the reigning aspect of a mature life. As the representative of such a life, he is an excellent type of Christ. It is rare to find in the Old Testament such a complete and full type of Christ. Therefore, on the one hand, Joseph represents the reigning aspect of the mature life and, on the other hand, typifies Christ in a full way. Throughout the record of Joseph's life there are two lines: the line of the type of Christ and the line of the secret of the reigning life. In this message we shall consider further the line of Joseph as a type of Christ, and in the next we shall consider the line of the secret of the reigning life. In previous messages we have covered eight aspects of Joseph as a type of Christ. In this message we shall cover seven more aspects.

(9) Resurrected from the Prison of Death

Joseph typified Christ as the One resurrected from the prison of death (41:14; Acts 2:24). Christ was not arrested and cast into prison. Rather, He walked willingly into prison, that is, He went into the prison of death voluntarily. Although He entered into death willingly, the gates of Hades, which is the power of death, the authority of darkness, immediately rose up and sought to keep Him there forever. But as Acts 2:24 says, it was impossible for Him to be held by death. Christ stayed in the prison of death for three days. During those days, the power of death did its best to imprison Him. But Christ could not be held by death because He is resurrection

(John 11:25). Which is more powerful—death or resurrection? Resurrection is definitely more powerful than death. Thus, death could not hold Christ, who was not only life, but also resurrection. Therefore, Christ walked out of death. To Him, this walking out of death was His resurrection. As Joseph was released from the dungeon, so Christ was also released from the prison of death.

All Christians should be familiar with three things: the incarnation of Christ, the crucifixion of Christ, and the resurrection of Christ. I believe that we in the churches know these three matters.

(10) Enthroned with Authority

Joseph also typified Christ as the One enthroned with authority (41:40-44; Matt. 28:18; Acts 2:36; Rev. 3:21). On the same day Joseph was released from the dungeon, he was enthroned to be the actual ruler over the whole land of Egypt. In like manner, after Christ was resurrected, He was enthroned with authority. Acts 2:36 says that the crucified and resurrected Christ has been made both Lord and Christ. On the day of Pentecost, the Apostle Peter seemed to be saying to the Israelites who had rejected the Lord, "The One you rejected, put on the cross, and killed, God has raised up from the dead. Not only so, God has made Him the Lord of all." This refers to Christ's enthronement. What a great matter this is!

(11) Receiving Glory

When Christ was enthroned, He received glory (Heb. 2:9). Joseph also typifies Christ in this regard, for when he was released from the dungeon, he received glory (41:42). Joseph's opposers not only sold him and despised him, but cast him into a dungeon. In chapter forty-one the prison is called a dungeon. The living conditions in Joseph's dungeon were far worse than the conditions of the prisons in this country today. The dungeon into which Joseph was cast was a pit. Those who put him there did so with the intention that he would be severely distressed. But God lifted him up and not only placed him on the throne, but also gave him glory. You may be wondering how we can prove that Joseph received glory. The proof is in the fact that he was clothed with beautiful garments and made to ride in the second chariot of Pharaoh (41:42-43). His being clothed with fine linen was in contrast with his being stripped by his brothers of his coat of many colors (37:23). When people saw him clothed with such beautiful garments and sitting in Pharaoh's chariot, they must have realized that here was a man in glory.

(12) Receiving Gifts

When Joseph was released from the dungeon and uplifted to the throne, he received gifts (41:42). Christ also has received gifts (Acts 2:33). Many Christians know that Christ resurrected, ascended, and has been crowned with honor and glory, but not many know that after Christ's ascension, enthronement, and glorification He also received gifts. Acts 2:33 says that Christ received of the Father the promise of the Holy Spirit, which He has poured out. What Christ received of the Father was a gift. In ancient times, many centuries before Christ, the same thing happened to Joseph. Joseph was not only glorified, but also received gifts.

In his glorification Joseph was given three things: a golden ring, some garments, and a golden chain. The ring was put on his hand, the chain was placed on his neck, and the garments covered his entire body. These three items portray in a full way the gifts that Christ received in His ascension to the heavens, the gifts that He has passed on to the church. When the prodigal son came home, he received the first two gifts, the ring on his hand and the robe on his body (Luke 15:22). At that time he did not receive the golden chain, which was to be given later.

Ephesians 1:13 says that we have been sealed with the Holy Spirit. This indicates that the Spirit of salvation is likened to a seal. We know that we are saved because we have been sealed. Fifty years ago I bought a gold-edged, leather bound edition of the Bible. As soon as I got it, I put my seal in the front of it to indicate that it belonged to me. I was afraid that otherwise it might be lost and I would have no way to prove that it was mine. After my Bible was sealed, however, I could prove that it belonged to me. Likewise, before we were saved, we were among the common people. But on the day we received the Lord Jesus, we were sealed. The seal of our salvation is the Holy Spirit of God. From that time onward, we have had a seal upon us. Suppose my Bible could say, "I don't like Witness Lee. I would like to belong to someone else." But my seal in the Bible would keep it from belonging to someone else. In like manner, we may feel that we do not want to belong to the Lord and that we would like to go along with Satan. Nevertheless, one who has been saved and sealed can never get away from the Lord. Even if it were possible for you to go into hell, you would still bear this seal.

The ancient Egyptians used their ring as a seal. Whatever they sealed with their ring was something important to them. Thus, the ring, the seal, received by Joseph typifies the Holy Spirit received by Christ. At the time of Christ's ascension and enthronement, Christ received of the Father the Holy Spirit that He might use Him as a seal to put on all His believers. Whenever anyone calls on Him, He puts this seal upon him.

As a saved one, you have a living seal on you. Even if you were to go to a gambling casino in Las Vegas, you would still have this seal upon you, and it would make you feel that, because you belong to Jesus, you should not stay in such a place. As our Joseph, Christ has received the seal from the Father, and with it He has sealed us. Now this seal is within us and upon us.

The second of the gifts Joseph received was the garments. We believers need at least two garments, one for salvation and the other for victory, for reward. The prodigal son in Luke 15 received just one garment because he was simply a saved one. He had not yet become victorious. After we have been saved and have received the garment of righteousness to justify us, we need to go on to live a victorious life. If we do, then in addition to the garment of salvation we shall receive another garment.

Often I have pointed out that the queen in Psalm 45 has two garments (vv. 13-14): one corresponds to the objective righteousness for our salvation, and the other to the subjective righteousness for our victory. The New Testament reveals that we believers should have two garments. The first garment is seen in Luke 15, and the second is found in Revelation 19. The garment of salvation is good for us to be justified before the Father. But in order to attend the wedding feast of the Lamb we need another garment. Both garments are Christ. The first, the garment of salvation, is the objective Christ. It is Christ put upon us (Gal. 3:27), Christ given to us to be our righteousness (1 Cor. 1:30). When the prodigal son came back home, he was not qualified to sit down with his righteous father. He needed a garment of righteousness to cover him and to qualify him for this. This garment is the objective Christ as our righteousness, which justifies us before the righteous God. But after we have been justified, we need to live out Christ. When Christ is lived out of us, He becomes our subjective righteousness, not just something put upon us, but something lived out of us. This is the subjective Christ as the second garment. Christ has been given to us as these two garments.

Our Christ is the real righteousness before God. Apart from Christ, there is no righteousness in the universe. In this universe there is only One who satisfies all of God's righteous requirements, and this One is Christ. Although it may not sound logical, this righteousness has been given to Christ. You may wonder how Christ can be righteousness, yet have this righteousness given to Him. Nevertheless, this is the biblical way of speaking, and we need to learn to speak the biblical language. The unique righteousness in this universe is Christ; yet this righteousness has been given to Christ that He may put it upon His believers. Christ is the righteousness that has been put upon us objectively for our justification. This righteousness which has been given to Him by the Father has been passed on by Him to us. Furthermore, He is constantly giving Himself to us so that we may live Him out of us. This is wholly a matter of gift.

The matter of Christ being righteousness yet having righteousness given to Him involves the Trinity. If this righteousness had never been given by the Father to the Son, it would not be so legally effective. Although the unique righteousness in the universe is Christ Himself, without this righteousness being given by the Father to the Son, not even the Son would have the right to use it. Therefore, the Father gave it to the Son so that the Son might pass it on to His believers, firstly as the objective righteousness, then as the subjective righteousness. We all have received the first garment, and there is no problem regarding our salvation. We are saved and we shall spend eternity with the Lord. This is more certain than a policy from the most trustworthy insurance company. But what about the second garment? We cannot at the present time be as certain of this as we are of the first garment, for we may not have paid the necessary premium for this second policy. We need to gain the second garment so that we may receive the reward. Praise the Lord that both the objective garment and the subjective garment are gifts! Both have been given by the Father to the Son, and the Son has given them to us. If you asked me if I have these two garments, I would answer, "I certainly have the first garment, and the second garment is within me and it is in the process of coming out." You also have received the second garment and have it within you. Now you need to pray, "Lord Jesus, process Yourself out of me. Lord Jesus, come out of me to be my second garment." We all need this garment.

Related to the second garment is the third item, the golden chain placed around Joseph's neck. In the Bible a chained neck signifies a subdued will. When the children of Israel were disobedient, the Lord referred to them as a stiff-necked people (Exo. 32:9). It would be very uncomely for a person with a stiff neck to wear a golden chain. It would be beautiful, however, to see a golden chain on a neck that is bowed. The chained neck signifies a will that has been conquered and subdued to obey God's commandment. When your neck has been conquered and subdued in this way, it is chained. Have you ever seen a woman wearing a necklace while quarreling with her husband? I have. When I saw this, I said to myself, "You should take off that necklace. Since you are being stiff-necked, you should not be wearing a necklace." Even a man's necktie is a type of chain. There is an amount of refinement related to wearing such a chain. The golden chain on the neck signifies the Spirit for obedience. Acts 5:32 says that the Spirit is given to those who obey God. Hence, the Spirit is given not only as a gift for salvation, but also for obedience.

How I admire the sequence of the things in the Bible. If I had listed the gifts given to Joseph, I would have mentioned the ring first, then the chain, and finally the garments. When I was young, I was bothered by the fact that the garments are mentioned before the golden chain. But the sequence of the three gifts in verse 42 is according to the spiritual sequence. In the spiritual sequence we firstly receive the Spirit for salvation. This is the seal. Then we receive the garment of righteousness, and we begin to live out Christ. In order to live out Christ, we need to have a chain on our neck. This means that our neck must be conquered, subdued, and chained by the Holy Spirit. Oh, the Holy Spirit will chain you! It will chain your stiff neck and cause it to be soft and subdued. Many saints in the church life have had their necks chained.

This is even true of some of the teenagers among us. When I was a teenager, I had a stiff neck. Although my mother loved me very much, my neck was still very stiff. Many of you teenagers are like this. However, when you call on the Lord Jesus, you are spontaneously chained. The Lord puts His chain on your neck, and your neck is softened and subdued. Sometimes your disposition may cause you to be unhappy with your mother. Nevertheless, because your neck has been chained, it is no longer as stiff as it used to be. When your neck was so stiff, there was no chain on it. But today you have been chained by the Holy Spirit, chained by the Spirit for obedience. Thus, others can see on your neck the beauty of the Holy Spirit for obedience expressed in your submission. You have been subdued, and you are submissive to your mother and father. Someone may say, "When I am eighteen years of age, I will have my freedom." This is not the testimony of a person chained with a golden chain. One who has a chain on his neck is submissive to his parents and to his teachers. When your neck is chained, it bears a certain type of beauty, the golden beauty of the Spirit for obedience.

These are the gifts received by our Joseph and passed on to us. I can boast that on my hand I have a ring, that around my entire being I have a robe, and that another robe is coming out from within me along with the golden chain around my neck. Hallelujah, Christ has received gifts and He has passed all these gifts on to me! Now I also have received gifts in Him. All this is typified by Joseph.

(13) Becoming the Savior of the World,
the Sustainer of Life (the Revealer of Secrets)

Because Christ was resurrected, enthroned, glorified, and received gifts, He is the Savior of the world. As the Savior of the world, He is also the Sustainer of life and the Revealer of secrets (Acts 5:31; John 6:50-51). Joseph typified Christ in these three aspects, for these titles are all included in the name Zaphnath-paaneah given to Joseph by Pharaoh (41:45). This name firstly means the Savior of the world; secondly, the Sustainer of life; and thirdly, the Revealer of secrets. We all know that Christ is the Savior of the world. As the Savior of the world, He is the Sustainer of life and the Revealer of secrets. All these titles were ascribed to Joseph. Firstly, Joseph was the revealer of secrets, then the savior of the world. He became the savior because he sustained the life of the people.

Regarding Joseph's being the sustainer of life, the record of the Bible is marvelous. Pharaoh had two dreams, the first of cows and the second of ears of corn (41:1-7). Why did Pharaoh not dream of seven turtles and seven black stones? Both the cows and the grain are good for food. Today we enjoy eating steak, which comes from cows, and bread, which comes from grain. Here we see two kinds of life—the animal life and the vegetable life. We need to enjoy both kinds of life. According to the ordination in the Bible, before the fall man ate only of the vegetable life (1:29). After the fall, however, man was told to eat meat because of the need for the shedding of blood for redemption (9:3). Thus, after the fall, man had to take as his supply the vegetable life and the animal life. Actually, the animal life must come first, for the fallen ones need to be redeemed before they can enjoy life. At the Lord's table we see the bread and the blood. The blood comes out of the Lord's animal life for redemption, and the bread comes from His regenerating life. In the Gospel of John the Lord is likened to a lamb. In John 1:29 John the Baptist said, "Behold the Lamb." This is the animal life for redemption. In John 12:24 the Lord compared Himself to a grain of wheat falling into the earth to reproduce by regeneration. This is the vegetable life for regenerating. Both kinds of life are mentioned in Genesis 41.

As we consider this, we realize again that the Bible is truly a divine book. No human being could have composed it. The more I probe into the depths of the Bible, the more I am convinced that its contents are divinely revealed. Surely it is the Word of God. Who other than God could have written such a chapter as Genesis 41? Today, the life supply we receive from the Lord Jesus as the Sustainer of life includes both the animal life for redemption and the vegetable life for production. Hallelujah, day by day we are nourished in this way! Simultaneously Christ is both the Savior of the world and the Sustainer of life.

He is also the Revealer of secrets, the One who interprets dreams. Have you ever considered how many dreams the Lord Jesus interpreted when He was on earth? By dreams I mean revelation, the secrets He has revealed to us. He interpreted at least seven dreams in Matthew 13 and a number of others in Matthew 24 and 25. Truly the Lord is the Revealer of secrets.

(14) Taking the Church

In 41:45 we see that Joseph took as his wife Asenath, the daughter of Potipherah, priest of On. Joseph's wife was a heathen, an Egyptian. Joseph took her during the time he was rejected by his brothers. This also is a type portraying how Christ has taken the Gentiles as His wife during the time of His rejection by the Israelites. As He was staying with the Gentiles, He obtained a wife from among them.

In the book of Genesis we have seen three wives who portray the church: Eve, the wife of Adam; Rebekah, the wife of Isaac; and Asenath, the wife of Joseph. As the wife of Adam,

Eve portrays how the church comes out of Christ and is a part of Christ. She typifies how the church is the same in life and nature as Christ and eventually becomes one Body with Him. Thus, Eve typifies the church being a part of Christ, coming out of Christ, returning to Christ, and being one with Christ. Rebekah portrays the church as the called and selected one, the one from the same source as Christ. Isaac came from a particular source, and Abraham's servant was sent to that source to select and call a wife for Isaac and to bring her to him. This selected one was Rebekah. Asenath portrays the church taken out of the Gentile world by Christ during His rejection by the children of Israel. During the time of this rejection, Christ came to the Gentile world, stayed there, and received the church out of the Gentile world.

Of his wife, Asenath, Joseph begot two sons, Manasseh and Ephraim. The name Manasseh means, "Causing to forget." When Manasseh was born, Joseph said, "God hath made me forget all my toil, and all my father's house" (41:51). This indicates that with the birth of Manasseh Joseph forgot all his afflictions. When Manasseh was born, Joseph seemed to say, "Praise the Lord! He has caused me to forget my afflictions." This reveals that when the church is productive, Christ will declare that He has forgotten His afflictions. If in the gospel meetings of the church in Anaheim some fruit is produced, Christ will declare to the whole universe, "Manasseh! I have forgotten My affliction."

The name of Joseph's second son was Ephraim, which means "Fruitful" (41:52). When Ephraim was born, Joseph said, "For God hath caused me to be fruitful in the land of my affliction." With Joseph, instead of affliction, there was fruitfulness. When we preach the gospel and produce fruit, Christ will be happy and declare, "There is no more affliction. But look at all the fruit!"

(15) Supplying People with Food

Joseph supplied food to the famished people (41:56-57). As such a supplier of food, he typified Christ as the One who supplies people with food (John 6:35). Today, what a Supplier of food Christ is! He supplies food to the famished people.

MESSAGE ONE HUNDRED THIRTEEN 1455

As we read the story of Joseph, we find that it is inexhaustible. Although we may read it again and again, we cannot exhaust its riches.

LIFE-STUDY OF GENESIS

MESSAGE ONE HUNDRED FOURTEEN

THE SECRET OF JOSEPH'S RELEASE AND EXALTATION

This message is a parenthesis covering the secret of Joseph's release and exaltation.

I. JOSEPH BECOMING QUALIFIED IN AGE AFTER THE FURTHER SUFFERING OF TWO YEARS

When some read chapter forty, they may have the desire to speak to the Lord on Joseph's behalf and ask the Lord why He kept Joseph in prison for such a long time. Joseph was seventeen or eighteen years of age when he was first put into prison, and he was about twenty-eight years of age when he interpreted the dreams of his two companions in prison. Although he had been in the dungeon for at least ten years prior to the release of his companions, his own dreams still had not yet been fulfilled. Perhaps you would say, "Lord, this is too much. You have tested Joseph for ten years already. Why didn't You release him when You released his two companions? After Joseph had interpreted the dream of the cupbearer, he asked the cupbearer to remember him. But the cupbearer forgot Joseph, and nothing happened. Lord, it is easy for men to forget. But You are God, and You cannot forget things. Why did You keep Joseph in prison for another two years?" One day I was enlightened to see that Joseph remained in prison for another two full years (41:1) because it was necessary for him to reach the age of thirty (41:46).

Today many young people expect to be released from their cage as soon as they turn eighteen. But according to the Bible, we need to reach the age, not of eighteen or even twenty-eight, but of thirty. Those who served God as priests began to do so in a full way at the age of thirty (Num. 4:3). The ones under thirty were apprentices, not fully functioning priests

(Num. 8:24). When the Lord Jesus began to minister, He also was thirty years of age (Luke 3:23). Thus, if Joseph had come to the throne at the age of twenty-eight, he would not have typified Christ in this matter. He had to be thirty years of age. After I saw this, I was convinced that these further two years were necessary for Joseph to be qualified. If he had not stayed there for two additional years, he would have been under age.

Young people, no matter how long your trial may be, do not be disappointed. You need to recognize that your trial is of God. No one can be enthroned without being tried and tested. Although we like to be enthroned immediately, God would say, "The time is not yet. Do not talk to Me about enthronement. You need to be put into the dungeon." If you seek the Lord, the Lord will put you into a dungeon. Perhaps all who are around you—your wife, your children, the elders, and the brothers and sisters—intend to respect you; however, whatever they do only serves to put you into a dungeon. We have nothing to say about this. Without the dungeon, we cannot ascend to the throne. Do not be a dungeon dropout; stay in the dungeon until you graduate and receive the crown. You need the last two years.

Although I may have no intention of putting you in a dungeon and although you may have no intention of putting me in a dungeon, what actually happens is that we put one another into a dungeon. When you were married, did you intend to put your wife into a dungeon? Surely you had no such intention. But this is just what you have done. Unintentionally and unconsciously, we put others into a dungeon. My children have done this to me. Sometimes they tell me how much they love me, but within myself I say, "Your love puts me into a dungeon." Nevertheless, we need to say, "Hallelujah for the dungeon! Although I have been here for ten years, I need to stay another two years." Again I say, do not drop out of the dungeon. Stay there and stay there gloriously, with praises to the Lord, not with the gnashing of teeth.

Madame Guyon was one who could praise the Lord in her dungeon. She even wrote a poem in which she likened herself to a bird in a cage. Here is the first stanza:

> A little bird I am,
> Shut from the fields of air,
> And in my cage I sit and sing
> To Him who placed me there;
> Well pleased a prisoner to be,
> Because, my God, it pleaseth Thee.

Madame Guyon grew to love her cage, which was her dungeon.

If Joseph had not stayed in the dungeon for twelve years, he would not have been qualified to rule over the land of Egypt. For this, he had to be thirty years of age. Those twelve years in the dungeon accomplished a great deal for him, not through objective education, but through subjective suffering and discipline. Be patient; eventually you will be qualified to rule. But in order to be qualified, you need to stay in the dungeon for another period of time.

II. JOSEPH RELEASED FROM PRISON INDIRECTLY THROUGH HIS INTERPRETATION OF THE CUPBEARER'S DREAM

Now we come to my burden in this message. My burden is to point out that Joseph was released from prison through his speaking by faith. Joseph dreamed that he was a sheaf rising up and that his brothers were bowing down to him. Ten years went by, and still this dream had not been fulfilled. If this had happened to us, we would have been disappointed to the uttermost and said, "Forget about this dream. I'm through with being a dreamer and with hearing about dreams." If Joseph had done this, he probably would never have been released from prison. He was released from the dungeon by speaking. However, Joseph was not released at the time he interpreted the dreams of his two companions. He interpreted their dreams by speaking in faith. If I had been the one interpreting dreams for others, I would have been afraid they would ask about my own dreams, because I would have had the vision, but not the experience or the fulfillment of the vision. Thus, I would not have dared to say anything for fear that someone might say, "What are you talking about? Don't talk about dreams until your own dreams have been fulfilled. I don't believe in you." But no matter whether his dreams had been fulfilled or not, Joseph spoke boldly by faith. If he had been questioned, he might have said, "Yes, I have had two dreams. Although they have not been fulfilled, I still believe in them. Perhaps tomorrow they will be fulfilled." Eventually, by his speaking Joseph was released from prison. If he had not spoken to the cupbearer, there would have been no one to tell Pharaoh about Joseph. It was the cupbearer who brought the news to Pharaoh that there was someone in prison who could interpret dreams (41:9-13). Therefore, Joseph was released from prison indirectly through his interpretation of the cupbearer's dream.

I have experienced this myself. In 1957 I was somewhat troubled by a problem that had arisen in the churches in Taiwan. But one day the Lord showed me that I should forget about the problem and begin to speak concerning the kingdom and the New Jerusalem, telling people that the church life today is a miniature of the New Jerusalem. Thus, I began to speak boldly, first in Taipei and then in Manila. An elderly British missionary attended the meetings in Manila and heard my messages. After one of the meetings, he came to me and said, "Brother Lee, do you mean these things to be for today or for the future?" When I said that I meant both, he replied, "The New Jerusalem will certainly be in the future, but I cannot see it here today. How can you say that it is both present and future?" Nevertheless, I continued to say that it was both. He would not believe it, but I did. Eventually, he left the church life. This indicates that the more you say no to the vision, the more you will be out. You may say, "There is no such thing as the church life; this is simply Brother Lee's dream. Let's forget about it." But the more you say this, the more you will be out of today's church life. We need to say, "Hallelujah! Praise the Lord! I believe that the church life is here today." The more you say this, the more you will be in it. This is a dreamer's vision.

We all need to speak like dreamers. Do not wait until you have the experience before you speak. Speak first. Speak immediately after you have seen the vision and then you will have the experience. Andrew Murray once said that a good minister always speaks more than he has experienced. In a sense, a good minister must be a boaster. During the years I have been in this country, I have spoken so boldly about the church life that some might have thought that I was boasting. Regarding the church life, some asked me, "Brother Lee, does this work?" I answered, "Why not?" For those who have said that it was impossible to have the church life, it has been impossible. In 1962 we had our first conference in the United States. Immediately after that conference, I was invited to a brother's home in Whittier. One day my host asked me, "Brother Lee, do you intend to say that what you minister actually works?" I replied, "I can assure you that it does. I would even sign a guarantee to this effect." Whether or not the vision works depends upon your mouth. If you say, "No," it will not work for you. But if you say, "Yes," it will work for you, even though it does not work for others. It all depends on whether you say yes or no. If you say no, it will be no; and if you say yes, it will be yes. Concerning the dream, the vision, it matters a great deal whether we say yes or no; for either our yes or our no will come true.

III. JOSEPH GIVEN AUTHORITY DIRECTLY THROUGH HIS INTERPRETATION OF PHARAOH'S DREAMS

Joseph's speaking not only released him from prison, but also ushered him to the throne. Joseph spoke himself to the throne. He was given authority directly through his interpretation of Pharaoh's dreams (41:25-44). If I had been the one interpreting dreams for Pharaoh, I would have been very cautious, fearing that Pharaoh would ask me about my own dreams. I would have been afraid that Pharaoh might say, "You don't have any experience. How can I listen to your interpretation? Your dreams have not been fulfilled. How then can my dreams be fulfilled? Go away from me." Joseph, however, was bold to speak, to interpret Pharaoh's dreams, and through his speaking he was given authority. Do you want to be released? Do you want to receive authority? If you do, then you need to speak. The more you speak, the more you will be released. Do not say that you are not qualified to speak, for the more you say that you are not qualified and that you are in the dungeon, the longer you will remain in the dungeon. But the more you speak, the more released you will be. Release will come through your speaking. In our experience we have found that the more we speak, the more released we are. I cannot tell you how released I am through my speaking. When I return home after speaking in the meeting, I am happy and refreshed. My speaking releases me from every kind of imprisonment. I do not care about so many things, for I speak my way out of the dungeon. Learn to speak yourself out of your dungeon. The best way to be released is to speak.

If you want authority, you need to speak. Speaking is what gave Joseph his authority. His speaking not only put him on the throne, but it secured for him authority over all the land. The more you speak, the more authority you will have. Release and authority both come through speaking. Whether you are at home, at school, or at work, you need to speak. Every time you come to the meeting, you should speak. We should be speaking all the time. The more we speak, the more release we shall enjoy, and the more authority we shall receive.

IV. JOSEPH MINISTERING FOOD TO PEOPLE THROUGH HIS INTERPRETATION OF DREAMS

Through his speaking Joseph also became a supplier of food. He ministered food to others through his interpretation of dreams. You may say that you are poor. You are poor because you are silent. Why are you so silent at school, in your neighborhood, or in the meetings? Why do you not speak? You may say, "Oh, I don't have enough experience to speak anything. I've been in the church life for many years. At the beginning, I heard that the church life would be glorious. But now I don't feel that it is very glorious. Thus, I don't have the assurance to speak anything about the glorious church life." However, the less you speak of the glorious church life, the less you will be in such a church life. You need to speak contrary to your feeling. Say something that is not according to your feeling, but that is according to your vision. When you declare that the church life is glorious, you will be in the glorious church life you are speaking into being. If you say, "I don't have it," then you will not have it. But if you speak, you will supply others with food. By your speaking you will have the release, the authority, and the food. Hallelujah, this all comes through speaking!

From time to time over the years, certain ones have said, "Brother Lee, how do you get so much life? Every time I see you, you are refreshed and full of life." I answer that I am refreshed and receive life by speaking. If I were to go to a certain place and were not to speak, I would be ready for burial. However, when I speak, I am released, I receive authority, and I have the food to supply others. I can testify to all that because I do the most speaking, I am more released, I have more authority, and I have more food. Oh, we all must learn to speak! Do not speak according to your experience—speak according to your vision.

V. JOSEPH'S LIFE BEING A LIFE OF DREAMS

Joseph was truly a dreamer, and his life was a life of dreams. A victorious and overcoming Christian will always be a dreamer. You need to have dreams, and you need to interpret the dreams of others. Day by day, let us all speak according to our vision, according to our dreams. Furthermore, we must interpret the visions of others, and we must live according to our vision. We should not speak according to our feelings, but according to the vision. We are visionaries. Because we are visionaries, we do everything according to the vision. Although a certain thing has not yet come to pass, we speak according to what we have seen of it, and we find that our vision is being fulfilled.

When we compare Joseph with the other outstanding men in Genesis, we see that he is unique in dreams and in suffering. None of the seven other great men had as many dreams as Joseph had; Joseph was always involved with dreams. His life was also unique with respect to suffering.

Dreams require interpretation, and interpretation is a matter of speaking. Therefore, Joseph was constantly speaking. Through his speaking, all the dreams were fulfilled. Firstly, Joseph spoke himself into trouble. If he had not spoken about his dreams, he would not have gotten into trouble. His brothers hated him and sold him into slavery simply because he spoke about his dreams. If after having these dreams Joseph had been silent, there would have been no problem. His sufferings came from his speaking.

After the Boxer Rebellion, many saints in England prayed desperately for the vast country of China. The Lord answered their prayers by coming in and doing a marvelous work in the colleges throughout the country. Thousands of students, including a good number of brilliant ones, were captured by the Lord, and many of them saw a vision. I was one of these students, and I was very familiar with the situation. Brother Nee was not the only one to see something concerning the church. Many others did also. However, they were afraid to speak of their dream concerning the church. These students were afraid of the missionaries, whose goal was to advance their mission work, their mission church. They were fearful that if they spoke something different from what the missionaries were doing, they would get into trouble. Because of his bold speaking, Brother Nee was betrayed. In the middle 1920s he published twenty issues of a paper called The Christian. In the articles in this paper Brother Nee spoke according to his dream. As a result, people laughed at him, and he got into trouble. The missionaries, teachers, and theologians, all of whom were older than he, disregarded him and opposed him. Brother Nee had seen a vision of local churches in every city throughout China. A quarter century later, his dream was fulfilled. By 1948 there were about five hundred local churches in the provinces of China.

Before Brother Nee's dream was fulfilled, however, he suffered a great deal, not only from outsiders, but even from turmoil stirred up by insiders. Due to this turmoil, his ministry was set aside for a number of years. Brother Nee once told a certain brother that there was no possibility to ever resume his ministry. This is an indication of the severity of Brother Nee's sufferings. He suffered so intensely that he felt that it was impossible for him ever to resume his ministry. But, much to his surprise, the Lord did something in 1948 to restore his ministry. In the forthcoming biography of Brother

Nee now in preparation all this will be made clear. As a result of the restoration of Brother Nee's ministry, hundreds of churches were raised up in the cities of China. This was due to Brother Nee's speaking, to his sounding of the trumpet, and to that of a few co-workers who were faithful to him.

Let me give a testimony of our experience in Taiwan. When we first arrived in Taiwan, we found it to be a backward, primitive island. Nevertheless, we began to speak according to our vision. There were many missionaries there, especially those from the Southern Baptist denomination. With the mainland of China lost, they invested a great deal of money in their work on the island of Taiwan. Although we were small in number, we spoke according to our vision. This speaking of the vision caused trouble, for it stirred up opposition. Some said, "Are only you the church? What do you mean that you have the church life and that we don't?" Our speaking was strong. We published books and a little magazine entitled The Ministry of the Word, which has had more than three hundred issues. Today, through this magazine, we are still sounding the trumpet. During the past twenty-eight years, we have done a great deal of speaking. Our speaking has caused trouble, and we have suffered much opposition as a result.

However, whether the missionaries agreed with us or not, they eventually were subdued and had to admit that ours was the best work in Taiwan. In the church in Taipei alone there are more than twenty-three thousand members. Before our dream began to be fulfilled in Taiwan, we suffered a great deal. Although we suffered criticism and defamation, we never stopped speaking. The more others tried to keep us from speaking, the more we spoke. We kept on speaking ourselves into trouble.

As we have seen, Joseph firstly spoke himself into trouble. But later he spoke himself out of trouble and into the fulfillment of his dreams. All this happened through his speaking. Both the trouble and the fulfillment came by speaking. It is the same with us today. When we speak about the glorious church life, some may shake their heads in unbelief and wonder whether this can be worked out in the United States.

Some have even said that it is impossible. But it did work. During the past fifteen years in the United States, this dream has been fulfilled.

I first saw this vision fifty years ago, and wherever I have been—in China, in Taiwan, or in the United States—I have spoken according to it. Whoever has said no to this vision, to him it has been impossible for it to be fulfilled. But to those who have said, "Yes, it is possible," to them it has been possible. The more we say that the church is glorious, the more glorious it is. I believe strongly that the church in Anaheim will be glorious, for we shall speak ourselves into this glory. Be prepared first to speak yourself into trouble and then to speak yourself out of trouble and into the fulfillment of your dreams. These three things will happen to us all.

Some of you may be familiar with a slanderous book called *The God-Men*. The preface to this book was written by a man by the name of David Adeney, whom I met more than twenty years ago when he was engaged in a student work in the Far East. He appreciated our meetings, and he sometimes attended the Lord's table meeting in Hong Kong. Once he came to Taiwan to carry out a work on the campuses. He came to realize that our work at National Taiwan University was better than the work of others. Because our gospel preaching was so prevailing, he admired it. One day he came to see me and told me that our work on the campuses was very good and that he wondered whether or not we could work together. I told him that I respected his work for the gospel and that, as far as the gospel was concerned, we could work together. However, I pointed out that his goal was different from ours. The goal of our preaching was to build up the local church, but his preaching eventually would help the denominations. In our conversation I was very frank with him. I said, "Brother, you need to see clearly where we are and where you are. We have two different goals. Our goal is to build up the local church as the Lord's recovery; and your work would eventually help the denominations." In our conversation, according to what he told me, I said to him that he was out of Babylon, but only halfway to Jerusalem. He was not yet in Jerusalem. Recently I received a note from a young brother telling me that this

Brother Adeney had told him that in Taipei I once had said to him that he was out of Babylon, but not yet in Jerusalem. I was pleased to hear that he still remembered this word.

It is difficult for me to believe that such a brother, who expressed himself to me in a very nice way, could write the preface to the slanderous book entitled *The God-Men*. If I were speaking with him face to face, I would say, "Brother Adeney, don't you believe that we are God-men? How could you write a preface to a book defaming us in this matter?" In his preface he gave people a vague, ambiguous, negative impression about me. I feel very sorry for him that he became involved in such a defaming work.

All this trouble has come from my speaking. The opposition from Melodyland and the Bible Answer Man is the result of my speaking. Today I am still speaking myself into trouble. The more opposition there is, the more I speak. I am still speaking, and I intend to speak even more. I may speak myself into trouble, but the ones who oppose this speaking will suffer loss because of their opposition.

Suppose when the cupbearer and the baker told Joseph about their dreams, he did not have the faith or the boldness to interpret them. Joseph could have said, "You know, friends, more than twelve years ago I had two dreams. I interpreted these dreams, but even now I still have not seen them fulfilled. Now I don't know whether those dreams were real or not. I dare not say." Many who saw the vision of the church during the past fifty years held an attitude similar to this. Some said, "Brother Lee, we dare not say that what you are doing is wrong. We also have seen something like this, but we're not sure about it. Time will tell." If Joseph had expressed such an attitude to his companions in prison, nothing would have happened.

What do you suppose would have happened if Joseph had been uncertain in talking to Pharaoh? Suppose Joseph had said, "Pharaoh, I have had some dreams, but they have not been fulfilled. My interpretation of the chief cupbearer's dream has been fulfilled, but I don't know whether my dreams will ever be fulfilled. However, if you like, I will interpret your dreams for you." If Joseph's attitude had been like this, Pharaoh would have sent him back to prison. He would not have wasted his time with Joseph. But, although Joseph's dreams had not been fulfilled, he was bold to tell Pharaoh that God would give him an answer of peace (41:16). We all must learn to do this. Because of the vision, I cannot remain silent. When I speak, I am restful, joyful, and happy. The more I speak, the more released I am.

LIFE-STUDY OF GENESIS

MESSAGE ONE HUNDRED FIFTEEN

BEING MATURED
THE REIGNING ASPECT OF THE MATURED ISRAEL

(4)

To many readers of the book of Genesis, the stories of Joseph are like the stories told to kindergarten children. However, we must remember that in the book of Genesis the seeds of nearly all the spiritual truths are sown. Whether the record of Joseph is merely a series of kindergarten stories or the seeds of the divine truths depends upon our point of view in reading it. If we look at the record of Joseph's life from the point of view of a kindergarten child, we shall read it merely as a story for children. But if we see that Jacob had passed through so many tests and had become matured in life, we shall see that the record of Joseph is not merely a story, but a revelation of the reigning aspect of a matured saint. If we view the record of Joseph as being the reigning aspect of a mature saint, our understanding will be revolutionized. Genesis 42, therefore, which we shall consider in this message, is not a kindergarten story; it is part of the reigning aspect of a mature life.

What we see in the life of Joseph is the rulership of the Spirit. You may have heard of the regeneration of the Spirit, the conviction of the Spirit, the inspiration of the Spirit, the infilling of the Spirit, the anointing of the Spirit, the power of the Spirit, the light of the Spirit, and the life of the Spirit, but the term the rulership of the Spirit is something new. We all need to be under the rulership of the Spirit. This aspect of the Spirit is higher than any other aspect. It is even higher than the building of the Spirit. The rulership of the Spirit is the topstone, the capstone, of the structure of the teaching of the Spirit. The record of Joseph's life is a revelation of the rulership of the Spirit, for the rulership of the Spirit is the reigning aspect of a matured saint.

Two lines run throughout the record of Joseph's life: the line of Joseph as a type of Christ and the line of Joseph's personal life. We see these two lines in chapter forty-two. In order to have an adequate interpretation of this chapter, we need to consider both lines. We need to follow these two lines to the end of the record of Joseph's life. Both lines afford us light and nourishment. When I was a young Christian, I heard a great deal about Joseph being a type of Christ. However, what I heard only included the general points. Many details were left out, and certain chapters were even skipped. I also heard about Joseph's personal life, but the emphasis was mainly on those aspects of Joseph's life which could edify the young saints and teach them to be patient, forgiving, and loving. None of the messages I heard about Joseph used the term life. In this message we shall cover a number of matters pertaining to Joseph as a type of Christ. In the next message we shall consider more of Joseph's personal life. If we consider chapter forty-two carefully, we shall see that it gives a vivid portrait of Christ.

(16) Recognized by the Children of Israel

(a) The Whole Earth Being under Famine

Genesis 41:56 says, "And the famine was over all the face of the earth," and verse 57 says that "the famine was severe in all lands" (Heb.). At the time of chapter forty-two the whole earth was under famine. This is exactly the situation today. A famine is a severe shortage of food, the means by which human beings maintain their existence. Food, however, not only maintains our existence, but also gives us satisfaction. When we eat and drink, we do not merely have the sense that we are maintaining our existence, but that we are being satisfied. When I am filled with good food, I am happy. Thus, a famine actually denotes dissatisfaction. The whole world today is dissatisfied.

The nation of Israel in particular is experiencing such dissatisfaction. This nation is aggressively striving and struggling to maintain its existence. If you visit Israel, you will certainly sympathize with them, for they definitely need protection and safety to secure their existence. Israel seems to need the Golan Heights and the settlements along the Sinai wilderness to secure its existence. The reason the nation of Israel is striving and struggling is that it is under famine, under dissatisfaction. The United States, the leading country on earth, is in the same situation. It also is experiencing dissatisfaction. We need to apply Genesis 42 to today's world situation. If we do, we shall see that the entire world is in a famine.

(b) Food Being Only Where Christ Is

According to Genesis 42, food was to be found only where Joseph was (vv. 5-6). This indicates in type that food is only where Christ is. In other words, satisfaction can only be found in Christ. Where Christ is, there is satisfaction. Today, Christ is in the church. If you are in the church yet are not enjoying satisfaction, it indicates that you are in a famine. I can declare to all that I am not in a famine. Day by day I am nourished, filled, and satisfied with good food. Oh, the church is the land of satisfaction, the region of satisfaction, because Christ is here! Food, nourishment, and satisfaction are only where Christ is.

I truly sympathize with the nation of Israel. There is no need for them to struggle and strive or to negotiate with Egypt. They need to turn to Christ. The prime minister of Israel does not need to go to Washington or to Cairo; instead, he should carry out negotiations with Christ. If the Jews would call on Him, everything would be settled. Neither Cairo nor Washington can solve Israel's problem of dissatisfaction. The famine will end only when they turn to Christ and go where He is. Perhaps some saints of Jewish origin should write a letter to the Israeli prime minister telling him that the only person who can solve Israel's problems and give satisfaction is Christ. Some day the Jews will turn to the Lord Jesus. When they realize that all their struggles are in vain, they will be forced in their desperation to turn to Christ. Praise the Lord that we have taken the lead to turn to Him!

We are pioneers in this matter. More than fifty years ago I turned to Christ, having come to the realization that I was in a land of famine and that I was very dissatisfied. We who have turned to Christ have found food, nourishment, and satisfaction, for the food is found only where Christ is.

(c) The Children of Israel Forced to Turn to Christ

The Scriptures prophesy that the children of Israel will be forced to turn to Christ just as Joseph's brothers were forced to turn to him for food (42:1-5). Zechariah 12:10 says, "They shall look upon me whom they have pierced, and they shall mourn for him, as one mourneth for his only son, and shall be in bitterness for him, as one that is in bitterness for his firstborn." In Romans 11:26 Paul says, "So all Israel will be saved, as it is written, The Deliverer will come out of Zion, He will turn away ungodliness from Jacob." In the future, Israel will be forced to turn to Christ. Presently they are neither willing nor inclined to do this because they are ignorant of Christ. Although the prime minister of Israel is an intelligent man, he, along with all others in the Israeli government, is ignorant concerning Christ.

(d) Ignorant concerning Christ

Genesis 42:8 says, "And Joseph knew his brethren, but they knew not him." Just as Joseph's brothers were ignorant of him, so the people on earth today are ignorant of Christ. We, however, are knowledgeable regarding Him. Oh, we know Christ! We in the churches are not stupid. We know the world situation better than the political leaders do. We are at least as intelligent as the diplomats are, if not more intelligent. Because we are not stupid, but rather the most clever of people, we know where we must spend our time. The church is the best place for the young people to spend their time. When I was a teenager, I wasted time in so many activities. Eventually, I realized how dissatisfied I was and I turned to Christ. Now I am in the good land, the land of the church. I enjoy this land because Christ is here. We used to be ignorant concerning Christ, but now we are very clear regarding Him.

Whenever I read the newspaper, I realize that those diplomats discussing matters at the conference tables are, in the eyes of God, speaking ignorantly. They are altogether ignorant and foolish. All the conferences held in Geneva are filled with vain talk. It is much better that we come here and talk about the Bible. Our talk is most sensible, reasonable, logical, and even philosophical. Because we are no longer ignorant of Christ, we know what we are doing here.

(e) Christ Testing Them

We have pointed out that 42:8 says that Joseph knew his brothers, but they did not know him. Because they did not know him, Joseph tested them. This also is a type of Christ's testing Israel after they have been forced to turn to Him in ignorance. Today the nation of Israel is still struggling by itself. The Jews do not realize their need to turn to Christ. But after they have been forced to turn to Him, although in ignorance, Christ will put them to the test.

(f) Christ Disciplining Them

In 42:17-24 we see that Joseph disciplined his brothers. This typifies Christ's disciplining the children of Israel. Christ expects that the nation of Israel will turn to Him. But He is not loose or careless. When Israel is in the process of turning to Him, He will not only test them, but also discipline them. According to the prophecies in the Bible, the reformed nation of Israel will suffer many tests and endure a great deal of discipline. The Lord will chasten them that they may learn.

(g) Christ Showing Love to Them

As Joseph was disciplining his brothers, he loved them in a secret way (42:25). This secret love frightened them. According to the prophecies in the Bible, the Lord will also exercise His sovereign authority to provide for all the needs of the nation of Israel. There is no need to worry about Israel, for we have the assurance that the sovereign Lord will provide whatever Israel needs for its existence. For example, if the little nation of Israel needs certain territory, the Lord will give it to them. He has a way to do this, because He is King of kings and Lord of lords. He is higher than all the presidents on the earth. Whether or not Israel will retain the Golan Heights or the Sinai does not depend upon the decisions of presidents and diplomats. It depends upon the Lord's sovereignty. If I were a Jew living in the nation of Israel, I would rest in the Lord. I have no doubt that even today the Lord is extending His sovereign love to Israel in a secret way. The Lord will continue to do this on Israel's behalf in the future. If you read the newspapers, you will see this happening again and again.

The Lord will test and discipline Israel and at the same time extend His secret and sovereign love to them because He needs them. The record of Joseph's life in the book of Genesis reveals that Joseph needed his brothers. Whose need was greater? Did Joseph's brothers need him more, or did Joseph need them more? I would say that Joseph needed his brothers more than they needed him. Yes, Joseph had become the ruler in Egypt. However, Joseph was not yet satisfied, for he was still expecting to see the fulfillment of his dreams. In Egypt Joseph was very lonely and he longed to see his father and his brothers. He needed the fulfillment of his dreams, and he needed his father and his brothers. Thus, his need for them was greater than their need for him.

The principle is the same today with respect to the Lord Jesus. Whose need is greater—does the nation of Israel need the Lord Jesus more than the Lord Jesus needs the nation of Israel? I would say that the Lord's need of Israel is greater than Israel's need of the Lord. Likewise, we need the Lord Jesus and the Lord Jesus needs us. Again I would ask: Whose need is greater—do we need the Lord more than the Lord needs us? The Lord needs us more than we need Him. If you know this, you can tell the Lord, "Lord Jesus, how I thank You for taking care of my need. But, Lord, Your need of me is greater than my need of You. I may not care whether or not I go to hell, but You care about it very much." Do you dare to say this to the Lord? At least a few times I have said, "Lord, I thank You for Your care. But, Lord, I realize that You need me more than I need You. Lord, I know that You care about losing me." Whenever I have said this to the Lord, I have had the deep sense within that the Lord was smiling and very happy. He seemed to be saying to me, "O my little child, you know Me so well." We should not pray to the Lord out of the fear of being sent to hell. We should not say, "O Lord, I'm afraid I might be lost and sent to hell. Lord, have mercy on me and rescue me from hell. Oh, don't let me go to hell!" If you pray like this, the Lord may say, "What are you talking about? You are not so pitiful, and I don't need to have that much mercy upon you. I have already shown great grace to you. Don't you realize that I need you more than you need Me?"

(h) Ignorant of Christ's Love

Because the Lord needs the nation of Israel more than Israel needs Him, He loves them in a secret way. However, just as Joseph's brothers were ignorant of his love (42:27-28, 35), so the nation of Israel today is ignorant of Christ's love for them. We also have been ignorant of His love for us. I am somewhat concerned that many among us are still ignorant of the Lord's love. Are you clear about His love? Do you realize that you are not in the church because of your determination, but because of His love for you? The fact that you are in the church is the strongest proof that the Lord loves you. This does not mean, however, that the Lord Jesus does not love those outside the church. He certainly loves them, but they are missing His love. Although we may not be missing His love, we may be ignorant of it. I hope that from now on none of us will be ignorant of Christ's love. Rather, we should say to Him, "Lord, thank You for Your love. The fact that I am in Your presence is proof that You love me. Lord, how I thank You that I am here enjoying Your presence! Hallelujah for this sign of Your love!"

In this message we have covered eight aspects of the recognition of Christ by the children of Israel. If you consider the prophecies in the Old Testament and the New Testament, you will see that all these aspects are in the prophecies concerning Israel's relationship with Christ, their Messiah.

LIFE-STUDY OF GENESIS

MESSAGE ONE HUNDRED SIXTEEN

JOSEPH'S DEALING WITH HIS BROTHERS

In this message, another parenthesis in our life-study, we come back to the line of Joseph's personal life. I love the line of life even more than the line of Joseph as a type of Christ. As I was contacting the Lord with a praying spirit, the Lord showed me the points in chapter forty-two regarding Joseph's personal life which we shall cover in this message.

I. JOSEPH NOT OUT OF CONTROL IN SEEING HIS DREAMS FULFILLED

Joseph must have been very happy to see the fulfillment of his dreams. Chapter forty-two reveals that his brothers came to him and bowed down to him. Joseph was seventeen years old when he had his dreams. At the age of thirty he was exalted to rule over the land of Egypt. About nine years later Joseph's brothers bowed themselves down to him. This means that Joseph would have been probably thirty-nine years of age when his brothers came to him. Thus, about twenty-two years after his dreams, Joseph saw them fulfilled, but not until he had been betrayed and imprisoned. Then he spent many years in the dungeon and eventually was elevated to the throne at the time of his exaltation. But still Joseph did not see the fulfillment of his dreams. He had interpreted the dreams of his companions in prison and the dreams of Pharaoh, and the fulfillment of those dreams was a strong confirmation that his own dreams would be fulfilled. Nevertheless, Joseph had to pass through a long period of testing. It may seem to us that his patience would have been exhausted. Could you have waited twenty-two years for the fulfillment of your dreams? Joseph did.

Then on a certain day his brothers came and bowed down to him. If we had been Joseph, we would not have been able to contain our excitement. We would have jumped up and shouted, "Hallelujah! Don't you know that I am Joseph? How happy I am to see you!" We would have been beside ourselves with excitement. If the sisters among us had been there, they would have first wept and then embraced all the brothers. Joseph, however, was not out of control when he saw the fulfillment of his dreams. Rather, he was calm and his excitement was under control. He was able to control himself in such a way because he was a person with the rulership of the Spirit.

If you cannot control your own excitement, you cannot be a proper ruler. The ruling aspect of the mature life knows how to be calm, even in the most exciting situation. You may say, "Didn't Joseph weep when he saw his brothers?" Yes, he did. Joseph was a human being full of sentiment and normal feelings, not stone or wood. Nevertheless, even in his weeping we see that he was a person who ruled himself. Apart from Joseph, no one else could have controlled himself in such an exciting situation. But he conducted himself outwardly as if nothing had happened. This is the ruling life, the victorious life.

Often it is necessary for us to hold back our excitement. When Aaron's two sons were killed in the presence of God, Moses' words to Aaron implied that he should not weep, and immediately Aaron held back his tears (Lev. 10:1-7). Many times we also must hold back our tears and place ourselves under the rulership of the Spirit. A proverb says one who rules his spirit is better than one who takes a city (Prov. 16:32). The fact that Joseph remained calm under the rulership of the Spirit proved that he was the one qualified to carry out such a vast administration. Even in the most exciting of circumstances, he was not touched by any excitement. On the contrary, he remained calm, sober, and reasonable.

II. JOSEPH NOT HASTY TO SHOW HIS GLORY TO HIS BROTHERS

When Joseph saw his brothers bowing down to him, he was not hasty to reveal his glory to them (cf. 45:13). Not until his brothers' third trip did he reveal himself to them and expose his glory to them. Concealing our glory is even more difficult than holding back our excitement. You may be successful in restraining your excitement, but it is virtually impossible for anyone not to expose his glory. Joseph, however, was successful in this matter. He did not reveal his glory to his brothers immediately. This is another reason Joseph represents the reigning aspect of the mature life. He certainly had the qualifications of a ruler. Not until our self and our natural man have been thoroughly dealt with can we keep from revealing our glory to others. Joseph was a man who had been thoroughly dealt with and who was living under the rulership of the Spirit. Thus, he was qualified to be the reigning aspect of the mature life.

My burden in these messages is not merely to pass on teachings. It is to help you see the life in the book of Genesis and to know the way of life. The life manifested in the story of Joseph is not the human life, much less the fallen life. Moreover, it is not even the good natural life. Rather, it is the resurrection life, the life of God. Although Joseph was in an exciting situation, he did not display any looseness. This is life. With Joseph we see not only life, but also the way of life, which is to keep ourselves under control. Never think that Joseph was not human. He was full of human feelings and sentiments, but he kept himself with all his feelings under the rulership of the Spirit. Therefore, in Joseph we see not only the mature life, but a reigning life and the way of this reigning life. We all, especially the young people, need such a life and such a way that is the reigning aspect of a mature person. This life is not easily excited, and it does not reveal its glory. Instead, in the midst of excitement it remains calm, controls itself, and conceals its glory.

III. JOSEPH BEING WISE
IN DEALING WITH HIS BROTHERS

Joseph was very wise in dealing with his brothers. He was not at all loose. If I had been Joseph, I would have said to them, "Hallelujah, let us dance and have a feast! Let us be happy together." But Joseph did nothing like this. On the contrary, he was calm, sober, and wise. Joseph did not say,

"Reuben and Judah, you did what was right. But you, Simeon, were wrong, because you took the lead to put me into the pit. You need to be punished for this." Instead of saying such things, Joseph was wise in at least three ways.

A. Causing Them to Realize Their Guilt in Hating and Selling Him

Joseph put all his brothers into prison for three days. He did this for the purpose of causing them to realize their guilt in hating him and in selling him (42:21). If I had been Joseph, I would have put them into prison for three hours. I would have been too excited to keep them there any longer. I would not have been able to wait until I could feast with my brothers. Even if my brothers could have been patient, I would not have had the patience to wait three days. Three hours, however, would not have been adequate for Joseph's brothers to realize their guilt. They needed to be in prison for three days. During those days, they must have talked a great deal about what they had done to Joseph. Thinking that Joseph was not able to understand them, they even spoke in Joseph's presence about what they had done to him. But Joseph knew what they were talking about. How Joseph's brothers regretted what they had done to him! But Joseph seemed to say to himself, "Talk is not adequate. I should put them into prison so that they can become sober. Let them fellowship with one another in prison for three days and three nights." This was Joseph's way to cause his brothers to have a thorough realization of their guilt. When we are in a pleasant situation, it is difficult to realize our guilt and to repent. But if we are cast into prison, it is easy for us to repent and to condemn ourselves.

B. Disciplining Simeon

Joseph was also wise in his discipline of Simeon. In 42:19 and 20 Joseph said to his brothers, "If ye be true men, let one of your brethren be bound in the house of your prison: go ye, carry grain for the famine of your houses: but bring your youngest brother unto me." At first Joseph thought that one brother should be sent to bring the youngest brother and that all the rest should remain in prison. But after three days Joseph changed his mind and decided that only one should stay in prison and that the others should go to bring the youngest brother to him. Therefore, he "took from them Simeon, and bound him before their eyes" (42:24). I believe that it was Simeon who took the lead in plotting to murder Joseph. I also believe that Simeon took the lead to bind Joseph and to cast him into the pit. As 49:5-7 reveals, Simeon was a person given to anger. Thus, Joseph had him bound and put into prison. What do you suppose Simeon thought about there in prison? I believe that he repented to the uttermost and regretted what he had done. Perhaps he said, "Why did this man choose me? Why did he set his eyes upon me? Maybe it was because I took the lead in the plot against Joseph." Simeon was in prison for at least half a year, having been accused of being a spy. This was a serious crime and it could have cost him his life.

Do not think that Joseph was cruel and merciless for treating Simeon in this way. On the contrary, he was full of mercy. The ten brothers deserved their three days in prison, and Simeon deserved a longer period of imprisonment. Joseph was wise in doing this. He was controlled by a life that gave him a sober discernment. Whatever Joseph did to his brothers was right. He did neither too little to them nor did he do too much. We in the church life need to have such a life of discernment. If we have this discernment, we shall know what to do with the brothers and the sisters. We shall know how far we can go with them and where we need to restrain ourselves.

C. Testing Them with Respect to Benjamin

Furthermore, Joseph displayed his wisdom in testing his brothers with respect to Benjamin (42:15, 20, 36-37). In 42:15 Joseph commanded that the youngest brother, Benjamin, be brought to him. By singling out Benjamin in this way, Joseph helped his brothers to think about Joseph himself. If I had been Joseph, I would have said, "Don't forget what you did to Joseph." Joseph, however, wisely referred to Benjamin. As soon as he referred to Benjamin, his brothers were reminded of Joseph. This must have touched their consciences. In 42:13

they said to him, "Thy servants are twelve brethren, the sons of one man in the land of Canaan; and, behold, the youngest is this day with our father, and one is not." If I had been Joseph I would have asked, "Where is that one whom you say is not? What happened to him?" In his wisdom, Joseph touched his brothers' consciences.

IV. JOSEPH SHOWING LOVE TO HIS BROTHERS

Joseph's brothers were under his control, and he could have done whatever he wanted with them. If he had wanted them beheaded, he had the authority to command it. He also could have feasted with them if he had wanted to do that. But as one representing the reigning aspect of the mature life, Joseph behaved in a proper way toward everyone. Because not all his brothers were the same, he did not treat them all in the same way. The one who was the most evil required the most thorough discipline. As a type of Christ, Joseph did the same thing to his brothers that Christ will do to the nation of Israel in the future. First, Joseph disciplined them. In a sense, he terrified them. When I read about this as a child, I wondered why Joseph did not show love to his brothers. I thought that he should have immediately said, "I am Joseph, and you are my brothers. Let us embrace, dance, and have a feast." I wondered why, instead of showing love for his brothers, Joseph put them into prison. Joseph did everything soberly and with discernment. But this did not mean that he had no love for his brothers. On the contrary, he had a great deal of love toward them. However, at the time he could not openly display his love for them. Rather, he had to extend love to them in a secret way. He did this by restoring their money and by giving them provision for their journey (42:25). Because Joseph's brothers did not understand his wise dealing with them, they were frightened by his secret love.

I hope that the Spirit will speak more to you regarding these matters than I am able to utter. In the church life we need to learn to be calm and to restrain ourselves. We also need to learn not to show our glory. Moreover, we must learn to do things not in a careless and foolish way, but in a sober and discerning way. Finally, we also must have love for the brothers, even for those who require discipline. This is the life of Joseph. In the church life we need a calm life, a sober life, and a discerning life. If we have such a life, we shall know how to relate to the brothers and sisters. But whatever we do must be underlined with a secret love, a love that cannot be shown openly.

Verse 28 says, "And their heart went out, and they were afraid, saying one to another, What is this that God hath done unto us?" (Heb.). This was the response of Joseph's brothers when they found their money in the mouth of their sacks. When they found the money in their sacks, their heart went out, that is, their heart was exercised. They might have wondered about what had taken place in Egypt. They were terrified of what had happened there.

Joseph was a very sober person. I do not believe that anyone else could have done what he did. Genesis 42:9 says that Joseph remembered the dreams which he had dreamed of his brothers. Now, after twenty-two years, his dreams were fulfilled. If we had been Joseph, we would have forgotten everything in our excitement at seeing our dreams fulfilled. We would have said, "Now that our dreams have been fulfilled, let us forget everything else and be happy." But if Joseph had done this, enjoying to the uttermost the fulfillment of his dreams, he would not have been able to do anything to help his brothers. As far as he was concerned, he was ready to enjoy the fulfillment of his dreams. He did not need any more discipline. His brothers, however, certainly did need discipline. Thus, Joseph did not act for himself, but for his brothers. Rather, for their sake he was willing to sacrifice the enjoyment of the fulfillment of his dreams for a period of time.

Joseph's dreams were fulfilled in his brothers' coming to him and bowing down before him. If Joseph had intended merely to enjoy the fulfillment of his dreams, he could have said to his brothers, "I am Joseph, and I am so happy to see you. Let us eat together. Then you go back and bring my father here." Even in ancient times it would not have taken more than a few weeks for them to return home and to come back with their father. Joseph could have said, "I cannot wait any longer to be with my father. I've been away from him for more than twenty years. Now I want to enjoy his presence. I want to see him as soon as possible." No doubt Joseph desperately desired to see his father. But for the sake of his brothers he was willing to postpone his enjoyment. Joseph's sacrifice of this enjoyment caused him to delay the enjoyment of the fulfillment of his dreams for at least another six months. The brothers had to go home, exhaust the food supply, and return for more grain. Eventually, their father came to Egypt to see Joseph.

Suppose you were Joseph. Could you have waited such a long time? As the ruler, Joseph could have done what was necessary to have his father brought to him immediately. But he disciplined his brothers for their good at the sacrifice of his own enjoyment of seeing his father. I repeat, Joseph was a sober, disciplined person. His personal temperament and sentiment were absolutely controlled by life. He did not go along with his own feelings. Instead, his sentiments were under the control of resurrection life.

All those who take the lead in the church need such a life. Without this kind of life we do not know how to help others. If we do not have such a life, we shall contact people according to our feelings, according to whether we are happy or sad. But Joseph did not deal with his brothers according to his sentiments, but according to their need. If he had acted according to his desire to see his father, he would have had his father brought to him immediately. But in order to discipline his brothers, he delayed his enjoyment of seeing his father for at least six months. He sacrificed his enjoyment of the immediate presence of his father for his brothers' good.

Apparently Joseph was treating his brothers in a rough way. As the nine brothers were returning home, they might have said, "My, that man really was rough with us! How he mistreated us! We were not only misunderstood by him, but also mistreated." When they returned to their father, they did not return joyfully, although they had the food they required. Then they told their father the sad story of what had happened to them in Egypt. They did not realize that Joseph loved them in a hidden way. As we have seen, he loved them in a secret way by restoring their money and by affording them sufficient provision for their journey. Joseph had no thought of revenge. He considered only what would be good for his undisciplined brothers. Even in the enjoyment of the fulfillment of his dreams, he was not selfish. He did not care for himself, but for his brothers, and he paid a great price to perfect them.

Those who take the lead among the children of God need to learn this lesson. We should not contact the saints in the church life according to our sentiments, but according to their need. Like Joseph in his dealing with his brothers, we should be neither strict nor loose in contacting the saints. Do not think that Joseph was strict with his brothers. He was sober in dealing with them in order to perfect them, but he was not strict with them. Neither was he loose, saying, "I forgive you all. I don't care about what you did, for I know that God sent me here. Let us just praise the Lord." If Joseph had treated them like this, there would have been no perfection.

According to his natural being, it was difficult for Joseph to put his brothers into prison for three days. He simply was not that kind of person. For him to do this was to go against his good nature. Nevertheless, in order to meet his brothers' need for discipline, he did this. In the church life we should not always be so kind. At certain times the leading ones need to be rough and tough. However, if you are rough with someone, you need to be rough in the right way. Otherwise, your toughness will kill him. The point here is that we should not deal with others according to our temperament, sentiment, or natural being. Neither should we deal with them according to our own enjoyment. Rather, we must contact others according to their need. Perhaps Joseph said to himself, "For the sake of my brothers, I must be tough and talk to them in a rough manner. I must put them into prison for three days." Like Joseph, we all must learn to deal with others according to their need and not according to our feelings.

The church life is similar to married life. According to God's ordination, there should be no divorce. Neither in married life nor in the church life should there be divorce. In the eyes of God, there is no escape, no emergency exit, from the church life. If you say that the church is no longer the church, it means that you are divorcing the church life. If five years ago you said that this was the church, how can you say that it is not the church today? How could you claim that a certain man is not your husband if you have been living with him for the past several years? There are many different kinds of people in the church life. It is not only difficult for us to remain together, but it is hard for a man to stay with his wife for a long period of time. Anyone who has done so can tell you that it is not easy. For this reason, this country is full of divorces. I once read statistics which indicated that in California there were nearly as many divorces as marriages. But there are no divorces among the young people married in the church life. We can boast to the demons that among the young people in the churches there is no divorce. Because the Lord's grace has been with these young people, they have learned to deal with their spouse, not according to their disposition, but according to resurrection life. In this matter of marriage we have enjoyed great success.

In the church life, however, we must admit that we have shortcomings. Although we have no divorces in our married life, in the church life sometimes the leading ones do not contact others in a proper way. We do not always contact them according to their need, but according to our sentiment, feeling, and enjoyment. In the coming years many young ones among us will be raised up by the Lord to take the lead. When they assume the lead, they must learn not to take the lead according to their sentiment, but according to the discernment that comes from being controlled by resurrection life. If they do this, they will contact the saints according to their needs and not according to their own sentiments. They will be like Joseph who dealt with his brothers according to their needs, even if he had to act contrary to his own desire for the enjoyment of the fulfillment of his dreams. In his dealing with his brothers, Joseph even went against his natural being. According to his natural constitution, he was not the kind of person to be rough with others. But because the brothers needed this kind of treatment, he dealt with them in this way. Joseph did everything according to the need of his brothers.

Not one thing he did was according to his desire, enjoyment, preference, or sentiment. Even in the matter of the fulfillment of his dreams, he ignored his feelings and took care of his brothers and of what would be good for them.

With respect to the leadership in the church life, we have not been altogether successful. By leadership I refer not only to the elders, but to anyone who takes the lead to help others. This includes those involved in shepherding. As we contact others in the way of shepherding, we must not do so according to our feelings. Rather, it should be according to the need of others. To learn this is to learn a great lesson. Joseph is an excellent example of proper leadership. He was a leader who did not act according to his need, desire, disposition, or sentiment. On the contrary, he did everything according to the need of others and for their good. When he spoke roughly to his brothers, it was for their good. When he put them into prison for three days, it was for their good. When he bound Simeon and kept him in prison for a longer period of time, it was for his good. We have seen that Joseph loved his brothers to the uttermost. However, he did not love them in a loose way, but in a sober way according to his brothers' need and for their good. We all need to practice this in the church life today.

LIFE-STUDY OF GENESIS

MESSAGE ONE HUNDRED SEVENTEEN

BEING MATURED
THE REIGNING ASPECT OF THE MATURED ISRAEL

(5)

The story of Joseph's being recognized by his brothers is the longest story in the book of Genesis, occupying three and a half chapters, from the beginning of chapter forty-two to the middle of chapter forty-five. When I was young, I thought that Joseph was too hard on his brothers. I thought that it was all right for Joseph to be hard on them the first time they came to Egypt to buy grain. As a man of God, he had the patience to discipline them, and for at least six months they underwent a trial. However, when they came to Egypt the second time, I thought that Joseph should not have done anything further to discipline them. According to my opinion, Joseph should have immediately revealed himself to them. However, Joseph did not do this.

For a long time I wondered about the reason for this. Certainly the first test of Joseph's brothers was necessary. We all agree with Joseph in testing them the first time. However, perhaps you also have wondered why Joseph tested his brothers again. On the one hand, he spread a feast for them and ate with them. But on the other hand, he gave them more trouble. What was Joseph's purpose in doing so? I believe Joseph expected his brothers to notice certain hints or indications and thus to recognize him. There should have been no need for Joseph to reveal himself to them directly.

In order to understand chapter forty-three, we need to remember that Joseph is both a type of Christ and also the reigning aspect of the mature life. Because Joseph was a type of Christ, we should not criticize anything he did. We are far below Joseph's standard. Whatever he did was the best, whether we agree with it or not. The Christ typified by Joseph could not do anything wrong. We would not do the same thing Joseph did because we are not as mature as Joseph was. We do not represent the reigning aspect of the matured life; we represent disobedience. This is the reason we do not agree with Joseph. However, if we came up to Joseph's standard, we would admit that what Joseph did to his brothers was the best. In his dealing with them there was no trace of childishness or foolishness. On the contrary, his dealings were wise and full of discernment. He dealt with his brothers so that they might be disciplined. Nothing he did to them was for his own benefit.

(i) The Children of Israel Further Forced to Turn to Christ

Just as Joseph's brothers were forced to turn to him again, so the children of Israel will be forced to turn to Christ (43:1-15). According to the Bible, the house of Israel will return to Christ at the end of this age and recognize Jesus of Nazareth as their Messiah. However, before they do this, they will need to be tested. The book of Zechariah reveals that the remnant of Israel will be put on trial. Even a good number of the Israelites will be killed. At the time the house of Israel turns to Christ, not very many Israelites will remain. They will be tested because they refuse to return to the One they need.

Consider the nation of Israel today. How they are struggling to protect themselves! Since 1918 I have been watching the world situation. Before the reformation of the nation of Israel, the Jews were scattered, and people paid little attention to them. Especially since 1967 the Middle East has been the focus of world news, the most crucial place on earth. Israel is opposed by nearly the whole world. Both the Arab countries and the United Nations condemn them. At times even the United States disagrees with Israel. Thus, she must fight for her existence. Israel is condemned by other countries because she has possession of the Golan Heights and the land west of the Jordan River. Israel insists on keeping these territories because she needs them to maintain her existence. However, if the nation of Israel would turn to Christ, everything would be solved. But Israel will not turn to Christ until she is forced to do so.

(j) Still Being Ignorant of Christ

Joseph's brothers were ignorant concerning Joseph (43:18-21), and the Jews today are ignorant of Christ. Joseph's brothers did not know that he was the ruler in Egypt. But their dissatisfaction due to the lack of food forced them to turn to Joseph. According to the prophecies in the Old Testament, the house of Israel will turn to Christ for no reason other than their need to maintain their existence. Apart from turning to Christ, there will be no way for them to exist.

It was the severity of the famine that forced Joseph's brothers to come to him again. The first time they came to Egypt they obtained some food on which to live. Thus, they returned home and stayed away from Joseph for another period of time. This is a portrait of the dealing of Christ with the house of Israel today. Unless Israel is forced to turn to Him out of their need to maintain their existence, they will never turn to Christ. Because the food brought home by Joseph's brothers was exhausted, and because the famine continued to be severe, they were forced to go again to the very one whom they did not want to see. I believe that after the first contact with Joseph his brothers had a bad impression of him. Perhaps they said, "If possible, we will never go back to that man. We don't want to see him again. He treated us very badly." The house of Israel is the same today regarding Christ. They do not want to even talk about Jesus Christ. Nevertheless, the steering wheel is not in their hands; it is in Christ's hands. At a certain time, they will return to Him.

Joseph was wise and very experienced. He did not allow his excitement at seeing his brothers or his desire to see his father to cause him to act foolishly. Rather, he was wise and calm, disciplining his brothers at the sacrifice of fulfilling his desire to see his father. If I had been Joseph, I would have revealed myself to the brothers as soon as they came to me the second time, and I would have told them to hurry back to my father and bring him to me. I would not have even taken the time to feast with my brothers before sending them back to get my father. But if Joseph had been like this, he would not have been qualified to be the ruler of the world. Joseph was a person full of wise discernment. Thus, he was a full type of Christ. Christ never does anything according to His excitement. The world situation is under His hand. The car is not being driven by any worldly leader, but by the Lord Jesus. He is managing the situation in the Middle East.

From the time Joseph's brothers first came to Egypt, they were undergoing a test. I do not believe they had any happy times after meeting Joseph in Egypt. They would not have been able to forget Simeon who was in prison there. They also realized that their supply of food obtained in Egypt was limited. They knew that one day it would be exhausted and that they would have to return to Egypt and face that man again. Their need for food forced them to return to him.

In order for Joseph's brothers to recognize him, they had to pass through a certain process. According to the prophecies in the Bible, the house of Israel will need to pass through a similar process in order to recognize Christ as their Messiah. Christ will deal with them again and again until the house of Israel is forced to turn to Him. There simply will be no other way for Israel to exist.

When Jacob charged his sons to go back to Egypt and buy more food, they told him that they could not return to Egypt unless the youngest brother, Benjamin, went with them. Without having Benjamin with them, they would not have had the boldness to face that man in Egypt. They realized that it would be useless for them to return to Egypt without him. What a test this was! Eventually, Jacob was forced to agree with this condition. Jacob seemed to say, "For the sake of your lives and the lives of your children, I am willing to sacrifice my youngest son. I give him to you. Go down to Egypt and buy food." Do you think that Joseph's brothers were happy as they were traveling from the land of Canaan to Egypt? Do you think that they were singing and saying, "Praise the Lord, we are going to Egypt again!"? Certainly not. On the contrary, all the way to Egypt they might have been saying to one another, "What shall we do with that man who put Simeon into prison? Probably the first thing he will do is put our youngest brother into prison. He may even seek a reason to take all of us as his slaves. Furthermore, he may seize our donkeys. What shall we do?" I am rather certain that Joseph's brothers were afraid of becoming slaves and of losing their donkeys, which undoubtedly were very dear to them. I believe that as they were traveling to Egypt they were trying to find a strategy to use in facing Joseph.

(k) Christ Showing More Love to Them

After the brothers came the second time, Joseph showed them love by feasting with them in his residence. Although they did not recognize him, he wanted to indicate to them that he was intimate with them, even as he was testing them. At the end time, Christ will do the same thing to Israel. On the one hand, He will test them further, while on the other hand, He will take care of them in love.

(l) Still Being Ignorant of Christ's Love

Although their Messiah will show love to them, the Israelites will continue to be ignorant of Christ's love. I am assured that Christ is for Israel. Whether or not we are for Israel means nothing, for we are mere men. But it is vitally significant that Christ is for Israel. However, Israel today is ignorant of Christ's love. Eventually, after they have been forced to turn to Him, Christ will be forced to reveal Himself to them. At that time the house of Israel will recognize Him as their Messiah.

Now we come to another parenthesis. My burden in this message is actually on the parenthesis. In 43:1-15 Joseph's brothers were still learning their lesson, and in 43:16-34 Joseph still left them under his test. Although he showed them love, he did not reveal himself to them directly. Joseph tested his brothers because he was trying to induce them to recognize him. Joseph's brothers were stupid. If we had been they, we would have recognized Joseph by the many indications of his identity. Let us now consider these indications.

When Joseph's brothers came back, Joseph did not say a word. Rather, he charged his steward to invite the brothers to his residence, the home of the ruler of the earth. If I had been one of Joseph's brothers, I would have said, "We are foreigners visiting this country. We don't deserve this much attention. Why would such a high ruler invite us to his home to eat with him?" Perhaps you would say that Joseph's brothers thought that he would trick them and make them his slaves. Perhaps they had this thought. At any rate, they did not appreciate Joseph's invitation, but rather were frightened by it. Thus, they told the steward that the last time they had purchased grain they had paid the money, but the money had been placed in their sacks. They told him that they had not done this. The steward said, "Peace be to you, fear not: your God, and the God of your father, hath given you treasure in your sacks" (43:23). The steward seemed to be saying, "It was not that your money was returned to you. It was a gift from your God and from the God of your father." After Joseph's brothers had visited him the first time, Joseph must have spoken to his steward about them, at least telling him that they were Hebrews and that he had come to Egypt from their land. He must have told the steward that they knew God and feared Him. Otherwise, how could an Egyptian steward have answered in such a way? From whom had the steward received this kind of knowledge? He no doubt had received it from Joseph. This was an indication to Joseph's brothers that someone in Joseph's residence knew their background. After indicating to them that there was no problem regarding the money, "the man brought the men into Joseph's house, and gave them water, and they washed their feet; and he gave their asses provender" (43:24). He also brought Simeon out to them. Thus, the problems regarding the money and Simeon were solved.

Eventually, Joseph came in and asked, "Is your father well, the old man of whom ye spake? Is he yet alive?" (43:27). No matter how much Joseph had disguised himself, there must have been some sign of affection in the way he asked about his father. Joseph was not a stone, but a man full of affection. The tone of his voice in asking about his father must have been an indication of who he was. Verse 29 says, "And he lifted up his eyes, and saw his brother Benjamin, his mother's son, and said, Is this your younger brother, of whom ye spake unto me? And he said, God be gracious unto thee, my son." After saying this, Joseph ran into his chamber and wept. At that point Joseph's brothers should have asked themselves, "What is this? Why does the ruler ask about our father in such an affectionate way? And why did he not finish speaking to our youngest brother? He went out and came back with his face washed. What does all this mean?"

Immediately after Joseph returned, he had his brothers sit before him, "the firstborn according to his birthright, and the youngest according to his youth" (43:33). The brothers wondered at one another. Certainly they should have realized by this indication that this ruler was Joseph. There must have been particular features in Joseph's countenance that they could have recognized, even after twenty-two years. If they had put all the indications together, they would have said, "This is Joseph." They should have remembered that Joseph was taken to Egypt, and they should have realized that this man was Joseph.

Verse 34 says, "And he took and sent messes unto them from before him: but Benjamin's mess was five times so much as any of theirs." There must have been a purpose in Joseph's giving Benjamin a portion five times greater than that of the other brothers. His intention must have been to indicate to his brothers that he was Joseph and that he loved his younger brother. If I had been there, I would have had the boldness to ask the man if he was Joseph. However, none of his brothers did this. Rather, they had no discernment.

With respect to our knowing the Lord it is exactly the same today. The Lord showed Himself to us and we saw Him, yet we did not know Him. He did many things for us with a good intention, but we were frightened by what He did. Everything He did was motivated by love, but we had evil thoughts regarding it all.

Joseph had a loving intention in inviting his brothers to his home for a feast. But they had the evil thought that he was planning to seize them and make them slaves. Verse 18 says, "And the men were afraid, because they were brought into Joseph's house; and they said, Because of the money that was returned in our sacks at the first time are we brought in; that he may seek occasion against us, and fall upon us, and take us for bondmen, and our asses." The money and the donkeys were veils that kept Joseph's brothers from recognizing him. The donkeys meant a great deal to them, but they meant nothing to Joseph. Later, when Joseph sent his brothers back to get his father, he sent chariots with horsemen. Their money and their donkeys meant something to them. These were all they had. They were also afraid of being taken as slaves. It is the same with us today. The Lord may be directly in front of us and He may have done a great deal for us, but we cannot recognize Him or what He has done. Rather, we are afraid. Joseph's brothers should have realized that the ruler of the world would not have cared about their donkeys. We are the same way. When we came to Christ and then into the church life, we might have wondered about our money, our security, or our family. Joseph's brothers were poor. But they were under the rich care of the ruler of the earth. If I had been there, I would have said, "Forget about the money and the donkeys. I want only Joseph. I love him." In knowing the Lord, we are all as foolish as Joseph's brothers. Instead of considering Him, we consider ourselves, our money, and our donkeys. Joseph's brothers should have turned their eyes on Joseph and looked at him. If they had done so, they would have realized that the man resembled Joseph. But for them to look at Joseph, they had to forget their money. However, they kept their eyes on their money and might have said to one another, "Don't you realize this is a lot of money? We must be careful not to lose it." I doubt that Joseph's brothers set their eyes on his countenance adequately. If they had done so, they would have recognized him. Levi might have said to Reuben, "I am quite sure this man is Joseph. Let us not be afraid, but be bold and ask if he really is Joseph."

Today there are not many who know the Lord in this way. However, there are a few who recognize the indications of the Lord's deeds and realize that what happened to them was of the Lord. In our knowing of the Lord, most of us are exactly like Joseph's brothers. We do not consider Him. Instead, we consider our money, our possessions, and ourselves. Joseph's brothers did not search for the reason that a high ruler would do such things for them. They were fully occupied with their own interests. They had no thought that the man who was dealing with them might be Joseph. It is the same with us. No matter how many good things the Lord has done for us, we still do not understand what the Lord is doing. The Lord does everything with a good intention, but we regard it as a curse. Even if we knew it was a blessing, we still would not receive it.

Joseph's brothers had no discernment. Even after he had seated them according to the sequence of their birth, they still did not realize who he was. They had become preoccupied even before they had left home to travel to Egypt. Joseph's heart was good, but their thought concerning him was evil. They were totally preoccupied by their evil thoughts. We would do the same thing if we had evil thoughts towards someone who, with a good intention, invited us to his home for dinner. Due to our evil thoughts, we might fear that poison had been injected into the food. Although we might not be able to refuse the invitation, we would be afraid to eat the food set before us. Our host's intention is love, but our thought is evil. Joseph's brothers were filled with such thoughts. These thoughts were the colored glasses that kept them from seeing who Joseph was.

In addition to all these indications of Joseph's identity, there are two further indications. Verse 32 says, "And they set on for him by himself, and for them by themselves, and for the Egyptians, which did eat with him, by themselves: because the Egyptians might not eat bread with the Hebrews; for that is an abomination unto the Egyptians." Three tables were prepared, one for Joseph, one for the Egyptians, and one for the brothers. This indicates that the Egyptians did not eat according to the Hebrew way. In what way do you suppose Joseph ate, in the Egyptian way or the Hebrew way? Certainly he must have eaten in the Hebrew way. Joseph's brothers should have recognized that here was an Egyptian eating in the Hebrew way, a way that was abominable to the Egyptians. Joseph ordered the tables to be set up this way in order to indicate to his brothers that he was a Hebrew.

The brothers should have considered that this ruler was a Hebrew. How stupid Joseph's brothers were! If I had been there, I would have said, "Levi, this man is a Hebrew. Furthermore, he is younger than we are. Look at his face. Isn't he Joseph?" Although Joseph spoke the Egyptian language, they should have recognized his voice and his intonation. Nevertheless, they still failed to recognize him.

Still another indication is found in verse 26: "And when Joseph came home, they brought him the present which was in their hand into the house, and bowed themselves to him to the earth." When Joseph's brothers were bowing down to him, they should have remembered his dream. Twenty-two years before Joseph had had a dream, and now it was being fulfilled. If you had been one of Joseph's brothers bowing down to him, you might have said, "This might be Joseph, the master of dreams." Although Joseph's brothers had heard about the dream and were in the fulfillment of the dream, they did not recognize Joseph.

Perhaps you are wondering why Joseph did not simply reveal himself to his brothers at that time. If Joseph had done this, he would have been very childish. He preferred to give them some indications to help them to recognize who he was. How sweet it would have been if they had recognized him! However, due to their preoccupations and stupidity, it did not happen this way.

All of us today are under the hand of our Joseph. What we should do and where we should go is up to Him. How long it will be before we come back to Him depends on how much food He gives us. If He gives us food to last ten years, then we shall return after ten years. But He will not give us this much. Rather, He gives us a limited amount to force us to come back to Him sooner. Joseph knew that his brothers would return after a certain period of time. He knew how many people there were in his father's family and he knew how much food to give them. They were under Joseph's control. Hallelujah, we today are under the Lord's sovereign hand! Do not worry about the present or the future. You are not under your own control, but under the Lord's control. Do not trust in your donkeys, that is, in your degree or in your job.

Your destiny is under the hand of the Lord Jesus, and your future is under His control. I would like to share with you the good news that the Lord is still lovingly and sovereignly caring for us. What He has done, what He is doing, and what He will do is all motivated by love. In love He is seeking to induce us to know Him through the various indicators He gives us. All that He has done are indicators to lead us to know Him. Do not remain preoccupied, setting your eyes on your money, your donkeys, or yourself. Look away to Jesus and set your eyes on Him. If you do this, you will see Him, recognize Him, and know Him.

I like this story of Joseph and his brothers because it portrays my situation in knowing the Lord. How stupid I have been! The Lord has always been good to me, but I have constantly been worried that I would be damaged or suffer loss. All that Joseph did to his brothers was motivated by love. It is the same with the Lord Jesus in relation to us. If we would consider our past before the Lord, our tears would begin to fall and we would say, "Lord, I realize that my past has been just like that of Joseph with his brothers. You have always been good to me, but I have not recognized Your love because I have been occupied by evil thoughts and by my own concerns. Lord, I had no concern for You, and I never focused my eyes or my attention upon You. Lord, forgive me and help me from now on to keep my eyes away from everything other than You. Lord, I don't care for anything, not even for the invitation. I care only for You and for being in Your presence. Lord, as long as I am here in Your presence, I am satisfied." This is the way to know the Lord.

If Joseph's brothers had been like this, with no preoccupations and no concerns for their money, their donkeys, or themselves, and if they had focused their eyes on Joseph, they would have seen certain features in his face which would have enabled them to recognize him. They also would have recognized him through what he had done for them. Hence, they would have said, "We should not forget that we sold Joseph into slavery in Egypt. Remember that his servants spoke of our God and our father's God. Also, we were seated at the table according to our birth. Moreover, consider the way this man treated Benjamin, and the affection in his voice when he asked about our father. When he spoke to Benjamin, he almost broke down and cried." How many indications there were to Joseph's brothers that this man was Joseph!

It is the same with us today in knowing the Lord. Do you think that the many good things that have happened to you have been accidental? No, they have all taken place with a purpose. But in the past we did not recognize what God was doing. May the Lord help us to know our Joseph. He has no evil thoughts toward us. Rather, His concern for us is a concern of love, and His intention is to induce us to know Him. The best thing is to know Him.

Even after Joseph's brothers had been dealt with so much, they still did not realize that they were meeting with Joseph. As we shall see in another message, their ignorance eventually forced Joseph to be patient no longer, but to reveal himself to them. My burden in this message is that we would be clear regarding the way to know the Lord. I can testify that many times the Lord has shown His love to me and has dealt with me in certain ways, yet I did not recognize Him or what He was doing. I was completely ignorant. But today we have a clear vision. Now we recognize Joseph and understand that everything He does is with the intention of helping us to know Him. May we all learn this lesson.

LIFE-STUDY OF GENESIS

MESSAGE ONE HUNDRED EIGHTEEN

BEING MATURED
THE REIGNING ASPECT OF THE MATURED ISRAEL

(6)

As we consider the story of Joseph, we need to remember that in his record there are two lines: the line of Joseph as a type of Christ and the line of life. It is difficult to find in the Old Testament anyone besides Joseph who was such a perfect type of Christ. He typified Christ in a detailed way.

(m) Christ Giving the Remnant of Israel the Last Test

In 44:1-13 Joseph gave his brothers the last test and gave them even more time to consider him. Christ will do the same thing to the nation of Israel. The prophecies in the Bible say that Christ will test the ignorant children of Israel, but they do not give the details. However, the record of Joseph's dealing with his brothers gives us a detailed picture of this. Even today the nation of Israel is ignorant of the fact that Christ is testing them. As we follow the world news, we should hold a view different from that of the worldly people. When I read the news, I am aware that what is happening in the Middle East is part of Christ's testing of Israel. The Israeli prime minister and his cabinet do not know that Christ is testing them. They claim to need the Golan Heights and the settlements along the Sinai to secure their existence. However, Christ knows better than they do what they need for their security. Do you not believe that what is happening to Israel today is a test? I certainly do. This is Joseph's testing of his brothers in order to teach them and discipline them. I expect this testing to continue year after year. The Lord Jesus Christ knows how to deal with the nation of Israel.

(n) Still Remaining Ignorant of Him

As Joseph gave his brothers a further test, they still remained ignorant of him (44:14-34). The same will be true of the nation of Israel as Christ continues to test them. What patience Joseph had! I do not have nearly the patience that he had or the patience that the Lord Jesus has with Israel today. If I had been Joseph, I would have revealed myself to the brothers much sooner than he did. And if I were the Lord Jesus, I would immediately tell the whole world that the Israelites are my brothers. Joseph, however, dealt with his brothers patiently. They were ignorant of him, and the Egyptians were ignorant of what was going on. Only Joseph knew what he was doing. The situation is the same today. Only the Lord Jesus, not the United Nations or the ruler of any country, knows what is taking place. Although He is giving the nation of Israel a difficult time, there is a definite purpose in all He is doing.

(o) Christ Acknowledging the Ignorant Israel

Eventually, Joseph acknowledged his ignorant brothers (45:1-4, 14-15). I believe that the time is near when Christ will acknowledge the ignorant nation of Israel (Rom. 11:26). The acknowledgment of the United Nations does not mean anything. What counts is Christ's acknowledgment. The day is coming when Christ will tell the world, "Don't touch the nation of Israel. Whoever touches her touches the apple of My eye. The Israelites are My brothers."

(p) Eventually Recognizing Christ

Joseph's brothers eventually recognized him (45:15), and the Israelites will eventually recognize Christ (Zech. 12:10). Until they recognize Him, Christ will continue to deal with them patiently. Recently I read that some Jewish scholars have begun to study the case of Jesus. It seems that these scholars are eager to learn more about who Jesus is. Instead of acknowledging the Jews now, Christ is giving them a further time to consider Him. These Jewish scholars who are studying the case of Jesus admit that Christ has gained a great deal of credit for the Jewish people, for Christ came from the nation of Israel. He was and still is a Jew. If Christ had come out of your country, you certainly would be proud of Him.

If we keep all these points in mind as we follow the news in the Middle East, we shall be happy and praise the Lord. All that is happening today was foreshadowed in Joseph's dealing with his brothers. In a sense, what we are seeing today is a motion picture of what has already taken place. Even as I am speaking about these chapters in Genesis, the events foreshadowed in them are taking place in the Middle East. What is happening today is the fulfillment of what is portrayed in this portion of the Word. Praise the Lord for His wisdom and patience! He knows what He is doing with Israel. In not too long a time, Christ will make an open recognition of the nation of Israel. He will do this by descending from the heavens to the earth. The Savior out of Zion will come to the land of Israel and recognize the nation of Israel as His nation.

Now we come once again to a parenthesis covering certain matters on the line of life. I love the line of Joseph as a type of Christ, but, as far as I am concerned, the line of life is more practical. The line of the type concerns Israel, but the line of life concerns you and me.

Although there were many clear indications of Joseph's identity, his brothers could not recognize him because of their blindness and preoccupations. Because his brothers were so blind and ignorant of him, Joseph was compelled to take a further step to reveal himself to them. Joseph must have prayed concerning his dealing with his brothers. He did not deal with them according to his personal feelings or desires, but according to the Lord's leading. Whatever Joseph did to his brothers was according to the Lord's leading.

No one else could have had the patience Joseph had. As we have pointed out, it took twenty-two years for his dreams to be fulfilled. After such a long period of time, Joseph had an intense desire to see his father. How could a man have had such patience? How could he have been able to control his emotion, his love, and his desire to see his father? Joseph's patience and self-control must have been of the Lord.

After the last test, at least one of Joseph's brothers, Judah, had improved. This is indicated by the way he spoke to Joseph about taking care of their father and their youngest brother (44:18-34). When Joseph's brothers sold him, they hated him and did not care for their father or youngest brother. Rather, they acted according to their hatred. But the way Judah spoke to Joseph indicated that he cared about his father and his youngest brother. This touched Joseph very deeply and convinced him that his brothers had learned their lesson. Thus, immediately after this, Joseph acknowledged them. Prior to this time, the brothers were still learning the lessons. The lessons were not completed until at least one among them had improved and had learned to care for his father and youngest brother. Until that time, Joseph exercised great patience in testing his brothers.

In my opinion Joseph should have revealed himself to his brothers immediately after feasting with them. However, he did not do this. Instead, he charged his steward to fill their sacks with grain and to return their money (44:1-2). No doubt Joseph's brothers were happy. If I had been one of the brothers, I would have said to the others on the way back to Canaan, "What do you think about that ruler? Why was he so nice to us? He is the ruler of the whole earth and we are foreigners coming to buy food. Yet he invited us to his home and feasted with us. He even gave Benjamin a portion five times greater than what he gave the rest of us. Moreover, he seated us according to our birth. What is this all about? Who is this man?" I believe that Joseph expected his brothers to talk like this. He expected them to thoroughly consider him. But they were careless and they did not do this. There must have been certain features of Joseph's face that would have enabled them to recognize him. But his brothers were too blind to notice them.

Suddenly, much to their surprise, the steward caught up with them and said, "Wherefore have ye repaid evil for good?" (44:4, Heb.). He then accused them of stealing Joseph's cup. The brothers replied, "Wherefore saith my lord these words? God forbid that thy servants should do according to this thing: behold, the money, which we found in our sacks' mouths, we brought again unto thee out of the land of Canaan: how then should we steal out of thy lord's house silver or gold?" (44:7-8). According to Joseph's plan, the cup was found in Benjamin's sack (44:12). This should have caused the brothers to wonder why that ruler in Egypt paid so much attention to their youngest brother. Joseph's brothers were terrified. As 44:13 says, "They rent their clothes, and loaded every man his ass, and returned to the city" (Heb.). When they saw Joseph again, "they fell down before him on the ground" (44:14). This also should have reminded them of Joseph's dreams. However, they still did not understand what was happening to them.

As we read this story, we see Joseph's patience and wisdom. Only a matured person has such patience and wisdom. The more matured we are, the more wisdom and patience we have. Although Joseph was just about forty years of age, in his spiritual life he was matured. Because he was spiritually mature, he had great wisdom and patience. Thus, he was not governed by his desire or emotion, but directed by his wisdom and patience.

In the church life today we all, especially the elders, need a life of wisdom and patience. What the elders do should not be under the direction of their emotion, desire, or intention. Although your intention may be very good, you may cause damage to others if you are governed by your good intention. None of the elders or leading ones in the church or in the work should be governed by his intention. On the contrary, we must be governed by our wisdom and patience. It takes no maturity to be directed by your intention or desire. But it does require maturity to be directed by patience and wisdom.

In the story of Joseph's revealing himself to his brothers we do not see any display of childishness on his part. Being full of patience and wisdom, he conducted himself according to the maturity of life. He was tried by his brothers' ignorance and blindness. But instead of being manipulated by his intention or desire, he was completely under the control of his wisdom and directed by his patience. In patience and wisdom he gave his brothers all the tests they needed. Because we are not as mature as Joseph, we may think that he was too severe and troublesome in dealing with his brothers. But Joseph was not a troublesome person; he was a person fully matured and governed by wisdom and patience. He knew what was the best time to reveal himself to his brothers. His acknowledgment of them was not directed by his desire or his feelings; it was completely under the direction of God's wisdom.

In wisdom, Joseph gave his brothers another test. By giving them this test, he gave them another opportunity to consider his identity. But, as we have seen, they remained ignorant. Therefore, he arranged for them to be brought back to him. When they returned, they were fully subdued. Judah said to him, "What shall we say unto my lord? What shall we speak? Or how shall we clear ourselves?" (44:16). When Judah spoke to him like this, Joseph still did not reveal himself to them, but continued to be patient, testing Judah to the uttermost. I do not say that Judah was mature in life, but at that moment he had improved very much. By the way he spoke to Joseph we see that he was a subdued, broken man. The attitude and spirit in which he spoke to Joseph about his father touched Joseph deeply. It was through Judah's talk with him that Joseph became convinced that his brother had learned his lesson. That was the right time for Joseph to reveal himself to them. At that time, all his emotions burst forth.

Do not think that Joseph was emotionless like wood or stone. No, he was full of emotion. Look at the way he wept when he revealed himself to his brothers (45:1-15). He told all his servants to leave the room, and then his emotions burst out. This indicates that Joseph was very emotional. Since he was so emotional, how could he have refrained from expressing his emotion for at least several months? The fact that he could do this was a sign of his maturity.

If we do not know how to control our tears, laughter, or anger, it means that we are childish in life. The strongest sign that we are matured is that we are able to control our emotion. As we pointed out in a previous message, when the two sons of Aaron were burned in the presence of God, there were indications that Aaron was forbidden to weep (Lev. 10:1-3). Aaron might have said, "My two sons have just died in my sight and you ask me not to weep. Moses, you are not human." Both Moses and Aaron were in the presence of the Lord.

Moses could serve God in His presence because he knew how to control his feelings of sympathy for his brother. Aaron took Moses' word. Whether or not you should weep, laugh, or be angry depends upon the Lord's presence. We are not in the world, but in the presence of the Lord in the Holy of Holies. When you are about to express your emotion, you should not do so according to your feeling. Rather, you must express your emotion according to God's presence. Does God's presence allow you to laugh? Does it allow you to weep? You should not say, "I have just lost my sons and I am very sorrowful. I simply cannot control myself. I must weep." If you say this, it reveals that you are not mature. Joseph could be the ruler in Egypt because he was mature. Being mature, he ruled over himself and over the whole earth. At the right time Joseph wept regarding his brothers. Even this reveals that he was a person fully under the control of God's guidance. In chapters forty-two through forty-four Joseph did not weep in the presence of his brothers. But in chapter forty-five, after the brothers had passed through the dealings and had learned their lessons, Joseph wept.

Joseph had been very concerned for his brothers. His concern for them is seen in the fact that he charged them not to quarrel with one another on the way home (45:24, Heb.). This indicates that they had been quarreling. Through the various tests Joseph exercised discipline over his brothers. Reuben or Levi might have said, "Throughout our entire life we were never disciplined as much as we were in these last months." They were disciplined by the patient and wise Joseph. Everything Joseph did in relation to his brothers was not for himself, but for them. In this we see Joseph's perfection in life. However, his perfection was not for himself, but for his brothers. He exercised patience and applied great wisdom. He constantly controlled his emotion and, prior to chapter forty-five, he did not weep regarding his brothers except privately after he had seen Benjamin (43:29-31). Although he had great emotion, he was not controlled by it.

In our married life we need to learn to control our emotion. Some say that to overcome our besetting sin is difficult. But this is not as difficult as controlling our emotion. To overcome your emotion is the most difficult thing. Are you able to control yourself when you are about to lose your temper? In this matter we all must learn of Joseph. When his emotion was about to burst forth at seeing Benjamin, he turned aside to weep privately and to wash his face. Likewise, if you are about to lose your temper at home, you should go to the rest room, let out your feelings privately, and then wash your face. Do not think that this discipline is for the older people but not for the young people. Joseph was still in his thirties when he exercised control of his emotions regarding his brothers. At the most, he was in middle age. Thus, you should not excuse yourself. Whenever you are about to lose your temper, remember what Joseph did.

When some hear this, they may say, "Brother Lee, didn't you say that the resurrection life within us is able to overcome everything? Why do we need to turn aside from others when we are about to lose control of our emotion?" The reason is that your natural life is so strong. I do not want simply to tell you the story of Joseph. My burden is that we would see the life Joseph lived. In Joseph's life his temper, disposition, emotion, intention, and desire were all under the control of God's leading. Joseph may have said, "God didn't lead me to acknowledge my brothers earlier than I did. I had no freedom to behave otherwise. I had to conduct myself according to the Lord's leading. I certainly wanted to reveal myself to them immediately and have them bring my father to me as soon as possible. But the choice was not up to me. It was a matter of the Lord's leading. I had to do what was best for my brothers. According to the Lord's leading, I had to put them to the test."

The result of the way Joseph revealed himself to his brothers was excellent and blameless. At the time Joseph revealed himself to them, the atmosphere was very good. In that atmosphere it was easy for him to forgive them. Actually, however, within Joseph there was not the thought of forgiving them. He fully understood that it was the sovereign God, not his brothers, who had brought him to Egypt. Because his dealing with his brothers was full of patience, wisdom, and self-control, the result was so excellent that he did not even need to forgive them. Realizing that God had sovereignly sent him to Egypt to fulfill His purpose, he spontaneously received his brothers. He embraced them and took them in.

When we are under the control of life in patience and in wisdom, we shall be like Joseph. We shall not blame or condemn anyone. There will not even be the need to forgive others because we shall not blame them. We shall be willing to accept everyone and we shall have a broad heart to embrace all the weaker ones, even those who have seriously offended us. However, instead of feeling that we have been offended, we shall realize that everything that has happened to us was according to God's sovereignty. Everything under God's sovereignty is for our good, for the fulfillment of His purpose, and for the edification of others. Because Joseph was sold by his brothers, good came to them. Through all their dealings with Joseph, the brothers were educated and edified. Therefore, the issue of the whole matter was excellent. Joseph not only carried out God's eternal purpose, but also built up his brothers. If we bring these matters regarding Joseph into our prayer and fellowship, we shall see more and we shall be nourished. Furthermore, we shall learn how to behave in every situation.

LIFE-STUDY OF GENESIS

MESSAGE ONE HUNDRED NINETEEN

BEING MATURED
THE REIGNING ASPECT OF THE MATURED ISRAEL

(7)

As we have pointed out many times, the book of Genesis contains the seeds of nearly all the truths in the Scriptures. If we would get into the depths of the record of Joseph's life, we must find the seeds sown there and see that this record contains an account of a reigning life. Before we consider the seeds and the reigning life found in chapters forty-five through forty-seven, we need to consider two further points regarding Joseph as a type of Christ.

(q) Christ's Revealing His Exaltation and Glory
to Repentant Israel

When all the tests were over and the time was ripe, Joseph revealed himself and his exaltation and glory to his brothers (45:8, 13). This typifies that one day Christ will reveal Himself to the remnant of Israel. Christ, the exalted One in the heavens, has His own temperament. He knows what He has to do to test Israel, and He knows how long the test should last. At the right time, the trial of Israel will end. After all the saints have been raptured and after the judgment at the judgment seat of Christ has been carried out, Christ, with the overcoming saints, will be revealed from the heavens, and the remnant of Israel will see Him. At that time they will realize who Jesus of Nazareth is and say, "Jesus of Nazareth is our Messiah. He has been exalted and enthroned as Lord of all."

When Joseph revealed himself to his brothers, they no doubt were shocked to see him and to remember what they had done to him. However, Joseph's revealing himself to them was wholly a matter of grace. Likewise, as a matter of grace,

Christ will reveal Himself to the remnant of Israel. At exactly the right time, Christ will reveal that He has been exalted and that no one in the universe is higher than He. When Joseph revealed himself to his brothers, he said that God had made him a father to Pharaoh, the lord of all his house, and the ruler throughout all the land of Egypt (45:8). Even Pharaoh was under Joseph's instruction. When Christ will reveal Himself in His glory to the remnant of Israel, the Jews will realize that He is far greater than they expected their Messiah to be.

(r) Israel Participating in the Enjoyment of Christ's Reign

After Christ reveals Himself to the remnant of Israel, He will begin His millennial reign. During the millennium, the Jews will participate in the enjoyment of Christ's reign, just as Joseph's brothers participated in the enjoyment of his reign (45:18; 47:4-6). Joseph's brothers enjoyed the best portion of the land in Egypt. This is a type of the millennium in which the Jews will enjoy the best things of earth. According to Zechariah 14:16-19, the Egyptians and those from the other nations will be required to present offerings to the Lord in Jerusalem. If a nation refuses to go up to Jerusalem with offerings for the Lord, no rain will fall upon their land. Because the Jews will be one with God, whatever is offered to Him will be their portion and enjoyment. According to the Old Testament, what was offered to God became the portion of the priests. In like manner, what is offered to God during the thousand years will become the portion of the Jews, who will be the priests instructing the people on earth, especially the Egyptians, in the way to worship God. I believe that during the millennium many Egyptians will repent for the way they dealt with Israel in this age. The Egyptians may say to the Jews, "We repent. We didn't know that you were such a people. Whatever we have that you want, just take it." This will take place according to the prophecy and the type in the Old Testament.

Now we come, once again, to a parenthesis regarding the matter of life. Remember, nearly everything in the book of Genesis is a seed. The first book of the New Testament, the

Gospel of Matthew, reveals Christ on the one hand and the kingdom of God on the other hand. Matthew also clearly indicates that we realize God's kingdom by denying ourselves. In Matthew 16 Christ, the church, and the kingdom are all revealed. In this chapter the Lord Jesus told His disciples that if anyone would follow Him, this one would have to deny himself. At the end of Genesis we find a seed of the truth of self-denial. In the closing chapters of Genesis, Christ is typified by Joseph, and the kingdom is foreshadowed by the house of Israel. Because Joseph denied himself, the kingdom of God could be realized in a practical way. The entire universe belongs to God, and God desires a kingdom. Although Pharaoh was ruling in Egypt, the kingdom of God was nonetheless realized through the reign of Joseph. The reigning of Joseph was the kingdom of God, which is for the fulfillment of God's purpose. According to the book of Exodus, the purpose of God is to have a dwelling place on earth. But at the end of Genesis we see a miniature of God's kingdom.

In all of history we cannot find anyone to match Joseph. Although he was offended by his brothers to the uttermost, he did not seek revenge. With Joseph, there was no thought of revenge. Rather, he denied himself and rendered the adequate and necessary discipline to his brothers. Joseph did not discipline his brothers for his own sake, but for their sake. Having no thought of revenge, he was concerned that his brothers might be perfected and built up so that they might live together as a collective people. The fact that Joseph charged them not to quarrel on the way home reveals his concern for them (45:24). The desire of Joseph's heart was that his brothers would be a people living together as God's testimony on earth. Joseph seemed to say to them, "I have done everything for you, and you have all you need. Now go back with thanksgiving to God to see my father and bring him back to me. But I am concerned that you might quarrel with one another on the way." Joseph's word about quarreling also indicates that he disciplined his brothers. He disciplined nine of the brothers in a general way and Simeon in a specific way. By this we see his discipline was sober; it was not motivated by anger.

Joseph was a person who denied himself. Whatever he did was based upon the principle of self-denial. I do not know of any other person who was offended to the degree Joseph was, yet who had not the slightest desire for revenge. When he revealed himself to his brothers, they were terrified (45:3, Heb.). Joseph, however, not only forgave them, but received them and comforted them. He said, "Now therefore be not grieved, nor angry with yourselves, that ye sold me hither: for God did send me before you to preserve life" (45:5). Here we see that the offended one comforted the offending ones.

Often when Christians forgive someone, they say, "Yes, I forgive you, but I also want to remind you of the seriousness of what you have done." This kind of forgiveness does not mean anything, for actually it is not forgiveness at all. When Joseph forgave his brothers, he comforted them and told them not to be angry with themselves, but to forget what they had done to him. He said that their selling him into slavery was God's doing to preserve life. Joseph did not blame his brothers for what they had done; rather, he regarded them as God's helpers. They had helped God to get him to Egypt.

In verse 7 Joseph said, "God sent me before you to preserve you a posterity in the earth, and to save your lives by a great deliverance." The Hebrew word rendered "posterity" is better translated "remnant." God's purpose required a remnant. His intention was that the descendants of Abraham, Isaac, and Jacob would build Him a tabernacle so that He might establish His kingdom on earth. If the remnant had been cut off, God's purpose could not have been fulfilled. In that case, the book of Genesis would have been the last book of the Bible. Knowing that the famine would have terminated everyone living in the land of Canaan, God prepared a way for the remnant of the chosen and called race to continue to exist.

Joseph was able to comfort his brothers because he realized that God, not they, had sent him to Egypt. He might have said, "Thank you for selling me. If you had not done that, how could I be here today?" Whether or not we forgive others depends upon our vision and realization. If we know that we are here for the Lord's recovery, we shall not care how much others offend us. We shall realize that the more we are offended, the more good will result. If Joseph's brothers had not sold him into slavery, how could his dreams have been fulfilled? His dreams were fulfilled through the ones who hated him. Joseph had a thorough realization of this and thus he could forgive his brothers for the way they mistreated him.

It should be the same with us today in the church life. If we realize that we are here for the Lord's purpose, for the Lord's recovery, then we shall know that whatever happens to us is for God's purpose. Romans 8:28 says, "And we know that God causes all things to work together for good to those who love God, to those who are called according to the purpose." Joseph loved God; therefore, whatever happened to him was for good. To be unwilling to forgive those who have offended you indicates that you are shortsighted. But if you see into the depth of what God has done, you will never seek revenge. Instead, you will always be willing to forgive those who have offended you. You will say, "Praise the Lord! Whatever happened to me was for good, not only for me, but for God's people. Whatever happens to me works good for the kingdom of God."

Joseph's realization that God was the One who had sent him to Egypt is a seed of the truth found in Romans 8:28. Joseph's life is an illustration of this verse and an example of how everything works for good for those who love God. The seed sown in the book of Genesis grows in Romans 8:28 and is harvested in Revelation 15, where we see the overcomers standing on the sea of glass, which signifies trials, tests, and sufferings. Joseph's brothers helped him come to the throne. If they had not sold him into slavery, he could not have come to Egypt. Hence, their selling of him ushered him to the throne. Do not complain about what your wife or husband or the saints in the church do to you. For those who love God, everything works together for good. The crucial matter here is whether or not we love God. If you love Him, even an accident works good for you. But if you do not love Him, not even graduating from a university with a doctorate will work good for you. I have suffered much throughout the years, but I have been comforted by the fact that everything works good for me.

Whenever I undergo suffering, I remember Romans 8:28 and I am comforted immediately.

As a young man of seventeen years of age, Joseph needed to undergo trials and testings. Because Joseph was the favorite of his father Jacob, he lived in a pleasant environment, and there was no way for him to suffer anything. He was always under his father's protection. But one day, according to the Lord's sovereignty, Jacob sent Joseph to his brothers, and they sold him into slavery. Through the sufferings that came upon him as a result of this, Joseph was trained to be a ruler. In this matter we see God's wisdom.

Firstly, Joseph had the dreams in which he saw his brothers bowing down to him. But in order for this vision to be fulfilled, Joseph had to undergo a great deal of suffering, especially at the hands of those closest to him. Joseph suffered constantly from the time he was seventeen until he was thirty. Joseph needed to pass through all these sufferings so that he might be perfected and qualified. God had sent Joseph to Egypt to preserve life so that a remnant might remain for the fulfillment of His purpose.

Do not be frightened by this word regarding Joseph's sufferings. Perhaps you have asked the Lord to make you today's Joseph. The Lord will answer this prayer by causing you to undergo certain sufferings. During times of suffering you may say, "How long, O Lord? The dreams of others have been fulfilled, but where is the fulfillment of my dream?" Eventually, you will be released. Joseph was patient and denied himself. He did not do anything for his own enjoyment, but for the discipline and perfection of his brothers.

In order to strengthen his brothers, Joseph revealed to them his exaltation and glory, and he told them that God had made him a father to Pharaoh. In 45:13 he said, "And ye shall tell my father of all my glory in Egypt." Joseph's brothers considered him like Pharaoh. But Joseph seemed to say, "I'm the father of Pharaoh. I am even higher than you realize, for God has made me the father of Pharaoh. You have seen all my glory. Go back and tell my father all you have seen." Joseph was not being showy. Rather, he was strengthening his brothers so that they might bring their father to him.

After suffering for thirteen years, Joseph was enthroned to be the ruler of the earth. He certainly longed to see his father. We may wonder why he did not do something to satisfy this longing as soon as he was enthroned. He could have sent chariots from Egypt to bring his father to him. However, it was nine years before he had Jacob brought to him. Joseph had the power and the position to do something, but he did not do anything. If I had been Joseph, I would have done something immediately. I would have taken an army of chariots and gone to visit my father. Had I found that he had died, I would have visited his sepulcher. Certainly it would have been normal for Joseph to do such a thing. The fact that Joseph did nothing about this for nine years does not mean that he had no thought of his father. Joseph was not stone or wood, but a living person full of emotion, a person who loved his father very much. Having been separated from his father for many years, he must have thought about him a great deal. He probably realized how close Egypt was to his father's home in the land of Canaan. He knew that the journey there would take just several days. Nevertheless, because he was under the sovereignty of God, he did not do anything.

Joseph preferred to remain under God's sovereign hand and not to initiate anything. He might have prayed, "Lord, it was You who sent me here, brought me through all the sufferings, and put me on the throne. It was You, Lord, who kept me from my father. Lord, I realize that all this has been of You. Thus, I dare not do anything. Rather, I would like to wait for Your sovereign time." I definitely believe that Joseph prayed this way. This reveals that he was a self-denying person. Although he had been enthroned to be the ruler of the earth, he nevertheless did nothing for himself or for his own enjoyment. He was wholly for God's interest. Joseph's life was a life that waited for God's sovereign timing. Instead of initiating the contact with his father himself, he remained continually under God's sovereignty, praying, "Lord, You do it. Unless You do it, I will not do anything." Young brothers and sisters, I expect the Lord to do much with you for His recovery. But you must learn the lesson not to go ahead by yourselves. Don't do anything on your own. Rather, keep yourself under God's sovereignty and let Him initiate something. Whatever needs to be done must be initiated by Him.

How sweet is the record of Joseph's life! Because Joseph was fully under God's guidance, there was no need for him to regret anything he did. Joseph is a living illustration of what is revealed in the New Testament. He was a self-denying person who had no self-interest, self-enjoyment, self-feeling, self-ambition, or self-goal. Everything was for God and for God's people. Therefore, when the time was right, he extended a warm invitation for his father to come to him.

We can learn many lessons by considering Joseph's life. Joseph had dreams and he interpreted his dreams and the dreams of others. All these dreams were fulfilled. Nevertheless, Joseph realized that he still lacked one thing, and that one thing was his father's presence. Humanly speaking, nothing could satisfy Joseph except the presence of his father. However, he did nothing of himself to secure his father's presence. Instead, he was patient, constantly waiting for the right time. For nine years he did nothing. Finally an opportunity came to do something. But, realizing that the perfection of his brothers had not yet been accomplished, he still did nothing. Only when his brothers had been edified did he extend the invitation. This invitation was initiated by God's sovereign hand. God sovereignly prepared the environment to indicate that the time was right for Joseph to send for his father.

When Joseph did send for his father, he himself did not go to get him. What was the reason for this? We cannot say that he did not have the time, for when his father died he had the time to bury him. In order to answer this question we need to discover what the Bible does not say. (This is one of the ways to study the Bible.) The reason Joseph did not go was that he was restricted. He did not want to do anything according to his emotion. Rather, his emotion was restricted. Joseph did not leave Egypt to see his father; neither did he send someone to find out whether or not a caravan was coming. In fact, Jacob "sent Judah before him unto Joseph, to direct his face unto Goshen" (46:28). Jacob seemed to be saying to Judah, "Judah, go to Joseph and tell him that I'm coming and ask him to direct us to him."

Do not think that Joseph was not eager to see his father. He certainly longed to see him. But even on the day of his father's arrival, Joseph was still at home. He did not make a special trip to meet his father on the way. Again I say that Joseph was a person fully under God's restriction. However, when he heard that his father had arrived in Goshen, he "presented himself unto him; and he fell on his neck, and wept on his neck a good while" (46:29). This proves that Joseph was very emotional and that he had a heart for his father. But he did not act according to his emotion; rather, he always acted under God's restriction. Because of this, he was able to be the ruler.

If you cannot rule yourself, you cannot be a good ruler. Suppose you lose your temper whenever you feel like it. If so, then you are through with the rulership of the Holy Spirit. But if we are under the rulership of the Spirit, we shall ask the Lord to have mercy on us when we sense that we are about to lose our temper. Only by being under God's restriction can we rule others. To be under God's restriction is the best discipline to prepare us for kingship in the coming age. No childish person, no one who has not been restricted, will be a king in the coming kingdom. In this matter of living under restriction, we see the maturity of life. May this word be a help to all who love the Lord, the recovery, and the church life.

In the Lord's recovery we have people from different backgrounds with different dispositions and concepts. Because of all these differences, we need to be restricted. If we are not restricted but express our emotion freely, we shall cause damage. We may regret later what we have done, but it may be too late. You may say, "I have the right to express my feelings like this." Yes, you have the right to do so, but you damage others. Do you want a proper church life? If you do, then you need to be under God's restriction. Consider again the picture of Joseph. He could bring in the kingdom only by being a person who denied himself. If he had acted according to his feelings and not according to God's guidance, everything would have been spoiled. But Joseph was a person wholly under God's restriction. Therefore, the kingdom of God could be brought in through him. In order for the kingdom to be realized in a practical way, there had to be a person who lived under restriction and who denied himself.

It is the same with us today. Do you want to have a pleasant church life? Then you must be under restriction and deny yourself. We all need to learn this. Suppose Joseph had not been a self-denying person. In such a case it would have been impossible for the kingdom of God to be brought in and realized in a practical way. Joseph's self-denial, his restriction under God's sovereign hand, was the key to the practice of the kingdom life. Thank God for Joseph's self-denying life. Through such a life God's purpose was fulfilled, and the kingdom was brought in, realized, and practiced. Through this fulfillment, the children of Israel shared in the enjoyment of the kingdom.

Joseph had the position and the power to do whatever he desired. However, he did not do anything for himself. More than forty years ago, I heard someone say that the strongest thing is to be able not to do something that you can do. You have the power, the position, and the opportunity to do a certain thing, yet you still do not do it. I became familiar with the story of Joseph many years ago. But in the past I did not see that after Joseph had been enthroned to be the ruler of Egypt, he did not use his power to see his father. After Joseph was enthroned, he did nothing to rescue himself from being alone, even though he had been separated from his father for thirteen years. When the brothers first came down to him, he still did not do anything. Joseph had the power and the position to do something about his situation, but he did not do what he had the power to do. This indicates that he was the most powerful person, one who has the strength not to do what he is able to do. Joseph was such a person because he was under God's hand, under God's restriction.

During the first nine years of his rule in Egypt, Joseph must have contacted the Lord again and again. Perhaps as he prayed to the Lord regarding the possibility of visiting his father, the Lord instructed him to do nothing about it. Week after week Joseph might have prayed, "Lord, is now the time for me to do something to have my father brought here?" I believe that the Lord said to him, "No, this is not the time. There is no need for you to do anything to fulfill your dream. Simply wait and allow Me to do it." By means of his prayer Joseph might have been confirmed in believing that his dreams were of God and that God Himself would fulfill them. Because there was no need for him to do anything, Joseph remained silent. He had the strength not to do what he had the power to do. When his brothers came to Egypt the first time, he did nothing to have his father brought to him. Even when the time was right for his father to come to him in Egypt, Joseph did not go out to meet him on the way. I believe that this was the result of his being under the Lord's restriction. Joseph knew that there was no need for him to do anything to fulfill his dreams. This is the real denial of the self and the genuine bearing of the cross.

To bear the cross means that you refrain from doing what you have the power to do. You are qualified and empowered to do everything necessary to fulfill your desire, yet you refrain from doing so. A person like this is the strongest person. The strongest person is not the one who is able to do something, but the one who is able not to do what he has the power to do. This self-denial is the unique way to usher in God's kingdom and to realize the kingdom life. As we shall see in the next message, the kingdom life came in through Joseph's ability not to do what he had the power to do. We need to be such people today.

There is no doubt that, in ourselves, we cannot be such people. Our life is not the kind of life that has the power not to do what it is able to do. When we have the opportunity to do something, we simply do it. But the life of Christ has the power not to do what it is capable of doing. This fact is the key to the four Gospels and to the life of the Lord Jesus. Often He had the position, the power, and the right environment to do many things, but he also had the power not to do those things. For example, He could have asked the Father to send twelve legions of angels to rescue Him; yet He had the strength not to do this (Matt. 26:53). This life of self-denial, of bearing the cross, is the life that ushers in the kingdom.

LIFE-STUDY OF GENESIS

MESSAGE ONE HUNDRED TWENTY

BEING MATURED
THE REIGNING ASPECT OF THE MATURED ISRAEL

(8)

As we have pointed out a number of times, in the story of Joseph there are two lines: the line of the type and the line of life. Before we consider further the line of life, we need to see another point regarding Joseph as a type of Christ.

(17) Reigning

Joseph was a type of Christ reigning in His kingdom during the millennium. If we take note of the prophecy in the story of Joseph, we shall see that his record is a picture of Christ's reign in the millennial kingdom.

(a) Supplying People with Food

According to this picture, Christ will do four things during the millennium. First, He will supply people with food, that is, He will satisfy everyone's needs (47:15-17). Although the whole earth was under a famine, Joseph was able to satisfy everyone's hunger. Today everyone is hungry and no one is satisfied. But when Christ is reigning during the coming thousand years, He will meet everyone's need and satisfy everyone's hunger.

(b) Keeping People Alive

As Joseph was reigning in Egypt, he kept people alive (47:19, 25). Because Christ will satisfy everyone's needs, He will be able to make everyone alive, to make everyone living. If you examine the prophecies regarding Christ's reign in the millennium, you will see that Christ will make everything living. Today, death is everywhere; everyone and everything is dying. But during the millennial reign of Christ, there will be hardly a sign of death. Rather, everything and everyone will be full of life.

(c) Keeping the Land Producing

Joseph also kept the land producing. He gave the people not only food, but also seed (47:19-23). In the millennium Christ will make everything productive. In today's situation, on the contrary, everything is diminishing. But when the millennium comes, everything on earth will be productive. In order to produce, we must have seed. While food is for satisfaction, seed is for production. As He reigns in the millennium, Christ will not only afford people food to satisfy them, but supply them with seed to make them productive.

(d) Taking Special Care of Israel

Joseph also took special care of Israel (50:21). This typifies that during the millennium Christ will take special care of Israel. Israel's specific function on earth is to testify of God. Although Christ is in favor of Israel, today Israel has no faith in Christ. The Jews worship God, but they do not have the proper faith in God through Christ. Instead, they believe in God in their own way. However, whether or not Israel is in unbelief, they are still the testimony of God, even today. There will be many nations on earth during the millennium, but only one nation, Israel, will be God's testimony. For this reason, Christ will take special care of Israel. When He renders this care to Israel, it will indicate that He is absolutely for God's testimony. Likewise, the reason Christ loves the church is that the church is God's testimony. Therefore, in the millennium Christ will satisfy everyone, make everything alive, make everything productive, and take good care of Israel as God's testimony.

Now we come to the line of life. When I first read that Joseph collected money, cattle, and land in exchange for food, I said, "Joseph, you are a robber. You not only robbed the people, you extracted everything from them. You collected their money, livestock, and land. Eventually, you collected their very being. Joseph, what kind of landlord are you?"

Joseph alone held the lifeline, and the lifeline was food. Those who wanted food had to give something to Joseph in order to get it. If they wanted satisfaction, they had to pay for it with money, cattle, or land. First Joseph "gathered up all the money that was found in the land of Egypt, and in the land of Canaan" (47:14). Verse 15 says, "And when money failed in the land of Egypt, and in the land of Canaan, all the Egyptians came unto Joseph, and said, Give us bread: for why should we die in thy presence? for the money hath ceased" (Heb.). When the people said this to Joseph, he told them to give him their cattle. Thus, the people brought their cattle to Joseph, and "Joseph gave them bread in exchange for horses, and for the flocks, and for the cattle of the herds, and for the asses" (47:17). A year later, the people came to Joseph again in need of food once more. This time there was no need for negotiation because there was a mutual understanding between Joseph and the people. The only thing they had left was their land and themselves. Therefore, they told him to buy them and their land for bread (47:19). Eventually, in Egypt Joseph was the only landlord, banker, and cattle raiser.

Joseph had the supply of life, the supply of food. According to our natural concept, Joseph should simply have given it away. But we should not bring our natural, worldly concept to the reading of the Bible. Joseph had the life supply, and the people needed it. They had to do something in order to get it. Before we see what the people had to do, we need to point out the reason Joseph became so rich and had the life supply. It was because of all his sufferings. From the time Joseph was seventeen years of age, he had been suffering. Even after he had been enthroned and was in power, he was still suffering because he was separated from his father. As we pointed out in the previous message, he had the power and the position to do everything necessary to have his father brought to him. But he refrained from doing so because he was in Egypt to fulfill God's will. In order for God's will to be fulfilled, Joseph had to suffer. Although he was the ruler, he suffered until the day his father was brought to him. Because of his suffering, he had the riches. It is the same today in the church life. It is those who suffer who are able to give others the supply of life. This thought is found in the hymn regarding the grapevine (*Hymns,* #635). The last two stanzas were arranged by Brother Nee:

> Not by gain our life is measured,
> > But by what we've lost 'tis scored;
> 'Tis not how much wine is drunken,
> > But how much has been outpoured.
> For the strength of love e'er standeth
> > In the sacrifice we bear;
> He who has the greatest suff'ring
> > Ever has the most to share.
>
> He who treats himself severely
> > Is the best for God to gain;
> He who hurts himself most dearly
> > Most can comfort those in pain.
> He who suffering never beareth
> > Is but empty "sounding brass";
> He who self life never spareth
> > Has the joys which all surpass.

If we do not suffer, we have nothing to give others. Because the grapevine undergoes many sufferings, dealings, cuttings, and breakings, it produces rich wine to cheer man. Brother Nee realized that the more we suffer, the more we have to give. Without suffering, anything we say is like tinkling brass. We may make noise, but there is no life in what we say. Therefore, as this hymn says, our life is measured not by gain, but by loss. Therefore, the reason Joseph could be so rich was that he had suffered. During the years of his suffering he stored up the riches.

During the seven years of plenty, Joseph stored up the grain. He did not take care of his own interests. It was not an easy task to store all that grain. For seven years Joseph gathered the grain and stored it in barns. This was a big job. On the one hand, Joseph was laboring; on the other hand, he was suffering because he was separated from his father. During these seven years he did not care for himself, but made arrangements for others to be taken care of in the future.

What he did in the seven years of plenty was for the people. He did this at the cost of taking care of his own interests, at the cost of seeing his father.

If we would be able to supply food to others, we must undergo a long period of suffering. Joseph did not have all the grain when he was seventeen years of age. He did not have the grain until he was thirty-seven years of age. At that time he became rich not in power, but in food and in the life supply.

It is the same today in the church life. The older, experienced ones have the supply. Again and again, Brother Nee stressed that we must take care of our physical life so that we shall not die at an early age. In one of his trainings Brother Nee asked the trainees what age they thought was the most useful age. Then he pointed out that a brother once said that the most useful age is from seventy to eighty. Because of this, Brother Nee charged the trainees to take care of themselves and not to commit gradual suicide. He told them to sleep well, eat well, drink well, and exercise well so that they might have a long life. When Caleb was eighty-five years old, he said that he was just as strong as he was at forty. The riches are not with the inexperienced ones. In order to be rich, we need to suffer for a long period of time. It took Joseph twenty years, from the age of seventeen to the age of thirty-seven, to become rich. Eventually, after many years of suffering, the food was in his hands. Because he had the food, all the hungry ones came to him.

According to my opinion, Joseph should have been generous with the people and said, "Whenever you need food, simply come to me and I'll give it to you." When I read Genesis 47 as a young man, I thought that Joseph was not generous. It seemed to me that he squeezed everything out of the people. I praise the Lord for showing me why Joseph was not generous. The reason is that the life supply should not be sold cheaply. If anyone in the church life is willing to give away the life supply in a cheap way, we must question whether the supply he has is genuine. The genuine life supply is never sold cheaply. Joseph seemed to be saying to the people, "Do you want the supply? If you do, then you must pay the price." The concept of generosity is a worldly concept. Joseph was in another realm, where there was neither generosity nor scarcity, just the supply and the price. Many Christians today sell things cheaply. But in the Lord's recovery nothing is cheap. If you want the food, you must pay the price. The greater the price you pay, the greater supply you will receive. Some today are opposing the Lord's recovery. But deep in their heart they know that this way is not wrong. They oppose it because the cost of taking it is very high. Thus, they take the cheap way and criticize the costly way. We cannot receive any food supply without a cost. Joseph will not sell you the food at a cheap price.

The people who came to Joseph for food paid four kinds of prices: their money, their cattle, their land, and themselves. How happy I am that the record in the Bible is so complete! These four items cover all the prices we need to pay today. When we pay with our money, cattle, lands, and ourselves, we receive all four types of supply. The first supply is not as rare or precious as the fourth supply. Each supply is more precious than the previous one, and the last is the most precious of all.

Let us now consider what money signifies. According to a superficial understanding, money is what we depend on. Actually, money represents convenience. The monetary system in this country is very convenient. In Joseph's time the people used silver. They had to carry silver with them and weigh it out when making a purchase. But today when we pay a bill, we simply write out a check for a certain amount. This is very convenient. However, when the supply in our checking account is depleted, we lose this convenience. At such a time we may worry about paying our bills. We all like to have a surplus in our checking account. But what will you do if this supply runs out?

Some are not willing to pay the price for the supply because they are concerned about losing their conveniences. Some may say, "Should I take the way of the church? Surely this way is good, but if I take it, I will lose certain conveniences. My wife or my relatives may be unhappy with me." But the more conveniences you give up, the more life supply you will have. Today's Christians, however, keep their conveniences, but have no life supply. In many cathedrals, chapels, and church buildings people hear messages every Sunday about conveniences. They go to these places to get more conveniences. For them, to take the way of the Lord's recovery is costly and inconvenient. Yes, if you take this way, you will lose your conveniences, but you will gain the supply.

The second item the people had to pay for the food supply was their cattle. It is easy to understand what is signified by cattle. Cattle signifies the means of our living. Joseph's brothers were concerned about their donkeys, worried that Joseph would find some excuse to take them away. Today you may care very much about your automobile. Perhaps you are afraid that it will be stolen. If so, your automobile is your donkey. For those with a doctoral degree, their degree is their donkey. For others their position is their donkey. But Christ, the rich One, the Supplier, is here, and He is neither generous nor stingy. Although He does not want to squeeze anything out of you, for your sake He requires that you pay a price. He will never sell His supply cheaply. After you pay your money, you need to pay with your cattle. Only by handing over your cattle will you receive the second supply. When both our money and our cattle have been handed over to Him, we shall be restful and at peace.

After handing over our cattle, we need to hand over our land. The land represents our resources. The Lord Jesus is a "robber"; He "robs" His lovers of everything. He takes our money, our cattle, and our land. He may say, "Give me your land. Do not keep the resources under your control, but hand them over to me." This is not a teaching, but an observation of what I have seen in the lives of many. Some dear ones were able to pay their money, but not their cattle. Others could give up their cattle, but not their land. Their concept was that the Lord Jesus always gives them things, but never "robs" them of things. But the Lord Jesus in His recovery "robs" us of everything—of our convenience, our means of livelihood, and our resources. If you are willing to give the Lord your lands, you will receive the third supply.

The last item the Lord requires is ourselves, including every aspect of our being. The Lord Jesus will claim every part of you. Have your ears been claimed by Him? If they have, you will not listen to anything other than Christ. Have your lips been claimed? If so, then they will be used differently. Has your whole being been claimed by the Lord Jesus? I doubt that very many have handed over their whole being to the Lord. Why are there still so many opinions, and why is there so little oneness and building in today's Christianity? It is due to the fact that very few are willing to hand themselves over to Christ.

Although you have heard many messages on consecration, you have probably not heard a message on handing yourself over to the Lord. Regarding consecration, we have been influenced by the Keswick Convention, which followed Mrs. Hannah Whitall Smith in emphasizing consecration as the key to everything. Do you want to be holy? Then you must consecrate yourself. Do you want to have your prayers answered and be victorious? Then you must consecrate yourself. But although we followed the Keswick teaching regarding consecration for years, we eventually discovered that it was not all that was needed for the life supply.

Consider what happened among us in 1948. Due to some confusion and turmoil, Brother Nee had to discontinue his ministry for a number of years. Some of us were burdened that his ministry be resumed, and we did our best to bring this about, but we could do nothing to help the matter. Before his ministry had been recovered, some of us had arranged to meet with him in his home for a time of fellowship. Although there were about thirty who wanted to attend that fellowship, Brother Nee would allow only me and two sisters to meet with him. He was not willing to sell his supply cheaply. Eventually, he allowed the others to sit in on the fellowship in a room adjoining his living room. The first morning no one said anything for a long period of time. Finally, unable to tolerate the silence any longer, I asked him to say a word about the confused situation of the churches in the provinces of Fukien and Kwangtung. In response, he poured himself out like Niagara Falls for more than an hour. His word was full of light, power, and impact. For at least six years he had not spoken a public word in that district, although a few had contact with him privately. Brother Nee's fellowship that day concerned the line of Jerusalem. (See the last chapter of *Further Talks on the Church Life*.) After he stopped speaking, no one said a word. Then one sister said, "Why don't we take Brother Nee's word and practice it?" With tears, everyone present said, "Amen! We want to practice it." Then Brother Nee replied, "If you intend to practice this way, you must hand over in writing yourself and everything you possess." My point in sharing this is that we need to hand ourselves over to the Lord. Perhaps you have consecrated yourself to Him, but have never handed yourself over to Him. Today Christ is claiming not only your money, cattle, and land, but also yourself.

By making the last payment, the payment of themselves, to Joseph, the people partook of the top portion. When you pay the first, second, and third price, you enjoy the first, second, and third portion. But when you pay the highest price, you enjoy the best portion. Eventually, we receive not only food for satisfaction, but also seed for reproduction. In order to get the food and the seed, we need to pay the full price. Before handing over ourselves, we must hand over everything else. After they gave everything to Joseph, the people could say, "Praise the Lord, we are released! We don't care for our money, cattle, land, or even ourselves. We just enjoy the rich supply." All that remained was the enjoyment. What a great blessing it is to give up everything for this enjoyment!

When the Lord Jesus comes, the whole earth will be under one landlord and one banker. All the land will belong to Christ, and we shall hand over whatever we have and whatever we are to Him. We are the enjoyers, not the lords. At that time in Egypt everything was under the hand of one lord. Joseph moved the people to cities "from one end of the borders of Egypt even to the other end thereof" (47:21) in order to have an even distribution. There were no rich and no poor. It is the same today regarding the spiritual supply. Christ has the riches. The amount of these riches that He is able to supply us depends on what we are willing to pay. If we are willing to make the first payment, then we shall receive the first supply. But if we are willing to make the other payments, we shall receive more supply. If we make the fourth payment, we shall receive not only the food to satisfy ourselves, but also the seed to produce something for others. How marvelous this is!

If you study Genesis 47, you will see that eventually the whole land of Egypt became a land of enjoyment. No longer were there distinctions between high and low and rich and poor. All the people became enjoyers on the same level because everyone and everything was under the same lord. This is a picture of the millennium. In the millennium there will be no capitalism or socialism. Everyone will be on the same level because everything will be under the Lord's hand. He will have bought everything, and He will have claimed everything and everyone. Truly the earth is the Lord's and the fullness thereof (Psa. 24:1).

The situation during the millennium will be very different from today. Before Joseph came to the throne, the people were on different levels. But after he was enthroned and the people came to him for food, Egypt became a prefigure of the millennium with all the people on the same level. Everything was under one man and belonged to him because that man had the riches and could claim everything. It must be this way among us in the church life today. Because Christ has claimed everything of us, we all are now on the same level enjoying the riches of Christ. All the points mentioned above also are seeds that are developed in the New Testament.

Joseph not only supplied the people with food, but also took care of his father's burial (49:29-31; 50:1-14). The burial of Jacob was not a simple matter. According to Hebrews 11, Abraham, Isaac, and Jacob all received the promise of the good land, but died without inheriting it. This is a strong indication of resurrection. Abraham died with the expectation that he would be resurrected. No doubt Isaac and Jacob had the same concept. Jacob died in the hope that one day he would rise up to inherit the land. For this reason, he charged Joseph not to leave his body in Egypt, but to bury him in the land of his fathers. Jacob realized that death to him was a time of sleeping and that on the day of resurrection he would rise up to inherit the good land. This is the significance of the burial of Jacob. The fact that Joseph buried him according to his request indicates that he had the same faith as his father. He also believed that they would rise up to inherit the good land.

Joseph also supported his brothers and comforted them (50:15-21). Joseph's brothers could not forget what they had done to him, and they were afraid that after their father's death Joseph would do something to get revenge. Joseph wept when he heard his brothers' request, for he had no thought of rendering evil to them. Rather, he said, "Fear not: for am I in the place of God? But as for you, ye thought evil against me; but God meant it unto good, to bring to pass, as it is this day, to save many people alive" (50:19-20, Heb.). Joseph also promised to support them and their little ones. Then he comforted them and spoke kindly to them (50:21). Joseph seemed to be saying to his brothers, "Your intention was evil, but God's intention was marvelous. He intended to send me here to save many lives. Please do not be bothered. I thank you for what you did to me. You helped God to fulfill His purpose." In the church life we need this kind of spirit. Even if others offend you, you need to consider that whatever they do to you is of God. If you take everything as of God, all the offenses will be over.

Joseph comforted those who had offended him. What grace he had! Because the offended one could comfort the offending ones, they could enjoy a pleasant life in the kingdom. Remember, Joseph and his brothers represented the people in the kingdom. Because of Joseph's excellent spirit, they could enjoy a good time together in the kingdom. But suppose Joseph wanted to render evil to his brothers. If such had been the case, the kingdom would have been an impossibility.

Like Jacob, Joseph died in faith. As he was dying, he charged the children of Israel not to leave his bones in Egypt, but to bring them into the promised land (50:22-26). This indicates that he expected the resurrection. He believed that one day he would rise up to inherit the good land and participate in all the enjoyment that would be there. Hallelujah for Joseph's victorious end! In the consummation of the book of

Genesis we see Christ, the kingdom, and all the aspects of the overcomers. How we thank the Lord for all this!

In the beginning of this book, God created man in His image to express Him, and He gave man His dominion to represent Him. After the experiences of so many called ones, this book concludes with a life that, in Jacob on the one hand, expressed God in His image and, in Joseph on the other hand, represented God with His dominion. How excellent and wonderful this is!

However, what is portrayed in Genesis was still a shadow in the age of typology. By Joseph's time the reality had not come. Hence, in this sense, Genesis concludes with a verse showing that Joseph died and was put in a coffin in Egypt. He died expecting the age of fulfillment in which he would share in the reality. In brief, as a whole, the book of Genesis begins with God's creation and ends with man's death and his being put in a coffin, even in Egypt. Because of the fall, death, the coffin, and "Egypt" are the destiny of fallen man. Thus, fallen man needs God's redemption, which is fully revealed and typified in the next book, Exodus.

About the Author

Witness Lee was born in 1905 in northern China and raised in a Christian family. At age 19 he was fully captured for Christ and immediately consecrated himself to preach the gospel for the rest of his life. Early in his service, he met Watchman Nee, a renowned preacher, teacher, and writer. Witness Lee labored together with Watchman Nee under his direction. In 1934 Watchman Nee entrusted Witness Lee with the responsibility for his publication operation, called the Shanghai Gospel Bookroom.

Prior to the Communist takeover in 1949, Witness Lee was sent by Watchman Nee and his other co-workers to Taiwan to ensure that the things delivered to them by the Lord would not be lost. Watchman Nee instructed Witness Lee to continue the former's publishing operation abroad as the Taiwan Gospel Bookroom, which has been publicly recognized as the publisher of Watchman Nee's works outside China. Witness Lee's work in Taiwan manifested the Lord's abundant blessing. From a mere 350 believers, newly fled from the mainland, the churches in Taiwan grew to 20,000 in five years.

In 1962 Witness Lee felt led of the Lord to come to the United States, settling in California. During his 35 years of service in the U.S., he ministered in weekly meetings and weekend conferences, delivering several thousand spoken messages. Much of his speaking has since been published as over 400 titles. Many of these have been translated into over fourteen languages. He gave his last public conference in February 1997 at the age of 91.

He leaves behind a prolific presentation of the truth in the Bible. His major work, *Life-study of the Bible,* comprises over 25,000 pages of commentary on every book of the Bible from the perspective of the believers' enjoyment and experience of God's divine life in Christ through the Holy Spirit. Witness Lee was the chief editor of a new translation of the New Testament into Chinese called the Recovery Version and directed the translation of the same into English. The Recovery Version also appears in a number of other languages. He provided an extensive body of footnotes, outlines, and spiritual cross references. A radio broadcast of his messages can be heard on Christian radio stations in the United States. In 1965 Witness Lee founded Living Stream Ministry, a non-profit corporation, located in Anaheim, California, which officially presents his and Watchman Nee's ministry.

Witness Lee's ministry emphasizes the experience of Christ as life and the practical oneness of the believers as the Body of Christ. Stressing the importance of attending to both these matters, he led the churches under his care to grow in Christian life and function. He was unbending in his conviction that God's goal is not narrow sectarianism but the Body of Christ. In time, believers began to meet simply as the church in their localities in response to this conviction. In recent years a number of new churches have been raised up in Russia and in many eastern European countries.

OTHER BOOKS PUBLISHED BY
Living Stream Ministry

Titles by Witness Lee:

Abraham—Called by God	978-0-7363-0359-0
The Experience of Life	978-0-87083-417-2
The Knowledge of Life	978-0-87083-419-6
The Tree of Life	978-0-87083-300-7
The Economy of God	978-0-87083-415-8
The Divine Economy	978-0-87083-268-0
God's New Testament Economy	978-0-87083-199-7
The World Situation and God's Move	978-0-87083-092-1
Christ vs. Religion	978-0-87083-010-5
The All-inclusive Christ	978-0-87083-020-4
Gospel Outlines	978-0-87083-039-6
Character	978-0-87083-322-9
The Secret of Experiencing Christ	978-0-87083-227-7
The Life and Way for the Practice of the Church Life	978-0-87083-785-2
The Basic Revelation in the Holy Scriptures	978-0-87083-105-8
The Crucial Revelation of Life in the Scriptures	978-0-87083-372-4
The Spirit with Our Spirit	978-0-87083-798-2
Christ as the Reality	978-0-87083-047-1
The Central Line of the Divine Revelation	978-0-87083-960-3
The Full Knowledge of the Word of God	978-0-87083-289-5
Watchman Nee—A Seer of the Divine Revelation ...	978-0-87083-625-1

Titles by Watchman Nee:

How to Study the Bible	978-0-7363-0407-8
God's Overcomers	978-0-7363-0433-7
The New Covenant	978-0-7363-0088-9
The Spiritual Man • 3 volumes	978-0-7363-0269-2
Authority and Submission	978-0-7363-0185-5
The Overcoming Life	978-1-57593-817-2
The Glorious Church	978-0-87083-745-6
The Prayer Ministry of the Church	978-0-87083-860-6
The Breaking of the Outer Man and the Release ...	978-1-57593-955-1
The Mystery of Christ	978-1-57593-954-4
The God of Abraham, Isaac, and Jacob	978-0-87083-932-0
The Song of Songs	978-0-87083-872-9
The Gospel of God • 2 volumes	978-1-57593-953-7
The Normal Christian Church Life	978-0-87083-027-3
The Character of the Lord's Worker	978-1-57593-322-1
The Normal Christian Faith	978-0-87083-748-7
Watchman Nee's Testimony	978-0-87083-051-8

Available at
Christian bookstores, or contact Living Stream Ministry
2431 W. La Palma Ave. • Anaheim, CA 92801
1-800-549-5164 • www.livingstream.com

Complete Set, Vols. 1-7, Catalog No. 10-217-001
ISBN 978-0-7363-0836-6

10-143-001
ISBN 978-0-87083-916-0